THE SYSTEMS THINKER

Essential Thinking Skills For Solving
Problems, Managing Chaos,

The Systems Thinker Series

ALBERT RUTHERFORD

D1521945

ISBN: 9798862300413

Printed in the United States of America

Email: albertrutherfordbooks@gmail.com

Gift

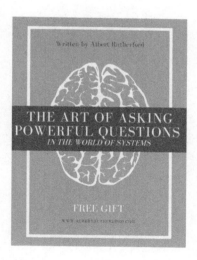

Visit www.albertrutherford.com to download your gift, The Art of Asking Powerful Questions in the World of Systems.

Contents

Introduction

"It isn't what we know that gives us trouble, it's what we know that ain't so." – Will Rogers

As humans, we are brilliant beings. This can be both a blessing and a curse. There are times when we revert to our "teenage ways" and think we know everything we need to about life when nothing could be further from the truth. If there is anything my time on Earth has taught me, it is how little I really know. I was responsible for educating adults and helping them get their start in the world until recently. I am acutely aware I couldn't teach my students everything they will need to know in their lives. The best I could hope for was to give them a thirst for knowledge and a love of learning, to inspire them to be lifelong learners. I planted the seeds of open-mindedness in their developing frontal lobe to receive and analyze new information even when it differs from their beliefs. I gave them the tools they need to find and recognize good reputable sources.

Many people think they have everything figured out and know all the answers. Take the Nazca civilization, for example. [1] They thrived in the desert ecosystem of southern Peru between 100 BC and 800 CE. Then they disappeared about 1500 years ago. While their disappearance has been a mystery, scientists now theorize that the choices they made as a civilization ultimately lead to their destruction. These tragic choices could have been avoided with a bit of humility and critical thinking.

The Nazca civilization lived in the desert where there was a delicate balance between living things that ensure survival. Despite having built a strong and successful civilization, they made a fateful decision that led to their decline. Their environment was home to the Prosopis pallida or huarango tree. This fantastic plant helped the soil to be more fertile and better able to hold in moisture. As well as support the irrigation system the Nazca had built. The huarango tree had the deepest roots of any tree in their area, which helped hold the soil in place and keep it from being eroded by rivers and wind. Also, as with all living things, it was part of nature's delicate balance.

The Nazca civilization's aforementioned fateful decision was to become an agricultural society. This may seem like a sound decision, but it led to a chain of unfortunate events. They made the transition to agriculture rather quickly, cutting down many of the huarango trees to make way for planting crops like cotton and maize. The mass eradication of the trees resulted in the decline of the natural benefits they had to offer. When storms like El Niño brought floods, their roots were not there to help hold the soil in place. The irrigation system didn't work well as the trees weren't there to keep the needed moisture in the soil to help their crops grow. The fertility of the soil gradually deteriorated. The Nazca were no longer successful in growing their crops. Food became scarce, there was not enough to feed everybody, so their civilization slowly disappeared as their people starved. [2]

One can't help but wonder if the Nazca had understood the science of the huarango trees and considered the long-term consequences of their choices, they might have made different decisions that would not have led to such a devastating outcome. [3]

The story of the Nazca civilization, while is tragic, is not unique. The history of planet Earth is rich with extinction stories and with choices that led to those extinctions. Again, we are brilliant beings. This sometimes is a blessing; other times, it is a curse. Usually, it is a curse for different species and generations who come after the perpetrators of environmental change. One man is not likely to see the long-term consequences of his actions in his lifetime.

How could the simple farmer of Mesopotamia or Mesoamerica know his accounting system and keeping track of his crops would result in e-books? How could the ancient scientist know that his experiment with metal alloys would result in the atomic bomb? To see the long-term impacts of these changes, thousands of years had to pass, and additional developments had to be made.

Life accelerated in the modern age. Thanks to science and engineering, changes have revealed themselves faster. For instance, biochemical and biological engineering helped increase the quantity of food available. Norman Borlaug was an agricultural researcher. He developed a high-yield type of wheat. It was so successful in Mexico, India, and Pakistan that it earned him the Nobel Peace Prize for preventing more than a billion people from starvation.[4] Genetic engineering has helped produce food at higher yields and promised a better life for our children. Physicists can create nuclear power to supply energy to our homes.

Let's take a closer look at the timeline of these innovations. The first biological engineering program started in 1966 at the University of California, San Diego. Genetic engineering, as we know it, being a direct manipulation of DNA by humans, has only existed since the 1970s. The first nuclear power plant opened its gates in 1954, in Obninsk, USSR.

We feel the benefits of these innovations today, even though they happened in our lifetime (the lifetime of fossils like me). What's even more impressive is that we have already started feeling the secondary impact of some of these innovations.

Pesticides created by biochemical engineering have killed pests only in the short term, allowing many to develop resistance. And at the same time, the number of other, untargeted insects such as wild bees dropped significantly.[5] Norman Borlaug, who has been considered the father of modern agriculture, got a lot of criticism from environmentalists and nutritionists. The Green Revolution produced many adverse side effects, such as increased cancer rates in rural areas, water, soil depletion, and fossil fuel dependence. [6] Due to the heat nuclear reactors release, the spawning pattern of fish in the affected areas has changed.

Not only science and engineering-related changes have accelerated to show their primary and secondary impact. Social, political, and economic changes operate at a higher speed too. It took hundreds of years to switch from a hunter-gatherer lifestyle to an agricultural-based society for our ancestors. How many years did it take to create a society where we can't imagine living without high-speed internet? Ten? I don't even want to talk about "internet" as a stand-alone term anymore. Could you imagine going back to dial-up? How have these developments affect us so fast? How did they affect the environment? And more importantly, what are the changes and consequences that are most likely to happen in the next twenty, fifty, or one hundred years? Future generations are all going to have kyphosis because we spend all our time hunched over the phone. I don't even dare thinking about a more distant future.

Had I been imagining the next hundred years in 1918, I would have never guessed what today would look like.

Traditionally, we have been taught to look at things in a linear analytical fashion to search for clear cause-and-effect relationships. If the car runs out of gas, the car stops. Easy, right? But how could we explain with the same logic the multidisciplinary changes nuclear power plants create? How could we tell that if the nuclear reactor releases heat, the spawning habits of fish will change? Can we explain this phenomenon purely through biology? Or chemistry? Or physics? No, we can't give a proper explanation with a reductionist, mono-disciplinary approach.

Systems thinking is a paradigm shift in the way we view the world. A system is a group of things that are interconnected and demonstrate their own behavior pattern over time. When we think in systems, we slow down and dig deeper, finding solutions and explanations to given phenomena. Systems thinking encourages us to look at events and patterns in our lives and around us; to focus our attention on the connection and relationship between the system's parts instead of only looking at the individual parts in isolation.

Systems thinking leads us from trying to come up with a quick fix to a problem in favor of considering the long-term consequences our actions may cause. It supports a deeper level of understanding than we typically take the time to seek.

In our fast-paced and complex society, the information we think we know can quickly become obsolete. We have to be open and receptive to new knowledge in science and technology and be willing to view it through our systems thinking lens. This way, we can rid ourselves of false information. We can be ready to face the future armed with the most accurate information available and make a more precise prognosis for the future.

Many of the significant issues I was tackling in my introduction aren't black and white. They have a lot of gray areas and multiple points of view to consider. For example, many people thought Norman Borlaug a hero. Some people believed his Green Revolution movement to be responsible for deforestation and devastating the soil in the areas his technique was practiced. Others disagree with bioengineering foods and argue that the region that was saved a million starvation death could also not economically support those lives. Borlaug circumvented a kind of cruel natural selection.

My point is that cases like Borlaug's aren't at either end of the extreme spectrum, the hero of starvation prevention or the cause of mass environmental deterioration.

Taking more viewpoints into consideration and examining them through systems thinking lens can prevent or rectify some tragedies. We can try to fix the most significant social problems with a higher chance of success. Ultimately, we can find more profound understanding and empathy in our experiences with other cultures.

Let's begin by taking a closer look at the evolution of systems thinking...

Where Is Systems Thinking Coming From?

Today's science has come a long way from where it used to be. In the past, science tended to look at events as individual occurrences that seemingly happened in isolation. Different science fields would concentrate on the event level without seeing how to fit it into the bigger picture. It is strange to carefully study, examine, and report on what you had observed about one puzzle piece without ever looking at the whole puzzle, isn't it? Well, pre-modern science functioned similarly.

Different fields of science have evolved throughout the years, and there has been a paradigm shift in data assessment. Scientists are still concerned with carefully examining individual events, but now looking at how it fits into the whole picture is also relevant. Things are more often interdependent than independent.

The world, in general, has drifted toward a scientific working-togetherness. Different specialties communicate with each other to cover every possible aspect of a given field of research. For example, you're studying a sub-tropical environment's soil erosion. To conduct proper research, you'd have an expert on vegetation, someone who can analyze soil samples, water samples, specialists for animals - both marine and land... All these professionals come together from different fields of science: biology, microbiology, geology, and so on.

You can see the same phenomenon in academia today. When a faculty member is going to take on a research project, they are never alone. The research includes at least some students to gather data and manage the project. Often, the faculty is working on the grant with other faculties. For example, the social sciences faculty can study the needs of refugees who may require special education services. The psychology faculty can devise mental support systems. The foreign languages department can provide information on the refugees' mother tongue.

Let's take a closer look at the changes major science fields have gone through over time.

PHYSICS

Classic physics focused on breaking things down into their smallest element to examine and study them. Physicists believed that these atomic pieces would act the same way whether they operated in isolation or as a part of a larger group. Things were viewed as a haphazard collection of atoms behaving determined by the laws of nature. The behavior was called "deterministic laws." This approach was later replaced by statistical laws rooting in Boltzmann's derivation of the second principle of thermodynamics.

Modern physics shifted its focus on problems of organization and how things may be interrelated.

Biology

Biology has been evolving in a very similar way as physics. In the past, biology aimed to break down living things to their smallest parts, cells, to be studied. Characteristics of organisms could be analyzed in isolation to understand how they worked, so they said. An organism is considered to be a multitude of cells working together. Organismic conceptions have gained greater importance as modern biology has evolved. It became crucial and necessary to study individual parts and the relation of organizations coming from interaction dynamics and behavior differences. Like physics, a more modern view of biology sees the value in learning how the parts of living things are interconnected and fit together in the bigger picture.

MEDICINE

Similarly, medicine was once most concerned with examining illness at the cellular level. There is value in that. Modern medicine, however, has evolved into seeing patients and their pain as a whole instead of merely zooming on their illness. Some doctors offer house calls. Patients can seek out a doctor who listens to them. The US medical schools teach bedside manners to young doctors to relate to their patients as people, not just a body on a table.

. . .

Sociology

Sociology, too, has undergone an evolution. It moved away from thinking about society as a sum of individuals who live within a given geographical circle. In the past, the classic economy defined society as the sum of its individuals. Modern sociology looks at a society, a country, or a nation as a whole which gives the basis of collectivism. This view can create unpleasant consequences as individual needs get "sacrificed" for the good of the community and country. Whether common good overpowers individual interests depends on the political zeitgeist of a given country. [1]

WHAT DO all of these scientific disciplines have in common? They have moved away from studying only the smallest parts of things to expanding their focus and include how those parts interconnect and interact. This is true whether objects of study are physical things, living things, or groups of people.

Many scientific fields shifted from deconstructing elements to their particles to analyzing their dynamics and working-togetherness. This shift seems to be present regardless of the scientific field. The question becomes, what is the driving force guiding these changes? Is there an isomorphic law[2] or guiding principle that extends beyond individual fields of science and connects them all?

The focus on examining whether identical laws run through all the different scientific fields is a relatively new approach. Until recently, it would have been virtually unheard of to look for similarities between atoms, molecules, people, bacteria, animals, and physical objects across all scientific disciplines. We are in the process of finding more similarities among them than we could have ever expected.

Where do these isomorphic similarities come from? Ludwig von Bertalanffy, the father of general systems theory, identified three reasons why different fields of study share the same isomorphic natural laws:

•There is a finite number of scientific laws for solving things. It makes sense that we use and adapt the laws available all across the scientific disciplines.

•We can apply these laws to our world.

•Natural laws, like the exponential law[3], can be true across a variety of scientific fields. They are valid in the same types of systems, even when the system elements are different.

LET'S take a closer look at how exponential law produces the same outcome across scientific disciplines. If the exponent is negative, the same rule applies to the decay of oxygen, the loss of body substance in a starving organism, molecular reactions, population decrease, financial decrease, or skill acquisition based on effort and time devoted. If the exponent is positive, exponential growth can be observed in all the areas above. The subjects involved in each scenario are different. The processes that lead to the general decay or growth are also different. Yet exponential law itself produces the same outcome in chemistry, biology, economics, demography, or individual skill acquisition efforts. [4]

The transition of thinking from part to whole across disciplines has made General System Theory possible. When Ludwig von Bertalanffy first established his famous thesis, he was hesitant to call it a theory. He didn't want to face the typical constraints of scientific theories of his time, confined to one field of science or area of study. He was examining systems as a whole and wanted to be free to use this view across multiple disciplines. He sought a more modern way of looking at the world and science to take a new, unifying direction.

Bertalanffy's theory was a new approach that came about during his studies following World War II. He focused on the similarities across all areas of science and didn't place more importance on one field over others. He recognized that the phenomena we observe in the world have much in common when considered a whole rather than just parts in isolation. He took a significant step toward the way we use systems thinking today.

THE GENERAL SYSTEM Theory had three main goals:

•To bring together the analytical way of investigating things and provide a scientific method for looking at the organismic domain by focusing on similarities between different scientific disciplines.

•To find connections between systems that, on the surface, appear to be very different but have a lot in common once analyzed deeper.

•To show that facts and values in science can and should harmoniously coexist in scientific investigations by adhering to a humane code of ethics. [5]

GENERAL SYSTEM THEORY sought to make generalizations about whole systems. It didn't want to abandon the foundation of knowledge of any field of science. It aimed to be transdisciplinary. Each field would bring its expertise to the table. They would actively engage in working together to create a common base of methods and for all scientific disciplines to share.

General Systems Theory wanted to "expand the tent;" to be more inclusive of knowledge from all areas. To stop being so focused on the little pieces that seeing the bigger picture becomes impossible. Bertalanffy didn't want to miss the forest for the trees.

Today systems thinking – while its methodology has changed and refined throughout the years - is actively used in politics, economics, sociology, demographic analysis, and environmental studies.

2

Today's Problems

When studying events, we look at them through analytical, logical lenses. We break them down into small, under-standable chunks, and we fish for scapegoats while looking for cause-and-effect relationships. Is the economy going south? It must be the result of the poor decisions of a politician. Is the newspaper arriving late? That lazy mailman. For sure, he stopped to chat with the neighbor. Is your wife cold and distant lately? It must be her job.

We seek linear, immediate, sensible explanations to problems surrounding us. But doing so, we run the risk of seeing issues as being inflicted upon us rather than looking for our responsibility in creating them.

We voted for the politician, after all. Or, if we didn't, what did we do to prevent their election? It was our choice to use one delivery service over another. And when it comes to our relationship, we have our mistakes in the mix.

Even if we assume personal responsibility for how our actions affected 'the system' we're only half way to understanding the picture as a whole. Our near-sighted view of the world focuses only on the areas closest to us, and the big picture remains fuzzy.

How can we zoom out? Interestingly, there were times when we had a more farsighted view. Before we even knew how to think logically, we were able to subconsciously operate complex systems. We are a complex system. We have intuitively built up our body-system with all its complexities. Our cells did this without any analysis or logic.

OUR BODY IS A SELF-MAINTAINING SYSTEM. We know we need hydration and food, but we don't think about how and when to digest, divide and absorb the nutrients, and so on. It seems we were born knowing instinctively how to relate to and understand complex systems.

Although systems thinking is relatively new as a discipline, its principles have been around for a long time. Some wisdom sprouted from our ancestors' heads a while ago. Let's look at a few examples:

Have you ever heard the proverb "A stitch in time saves nine?" This wise saying tells us that it is better to take a little time right away to deal with a problem. If we put it off, we might find that the problem has grown much larger and more challenging to solve. This idea is supported by systems thinkers. Escalation, for example, occurs when a situation goes unaddressed, and those affected get entangled in defenses instead of solutions. The butterfly effect shows us that an insignificant initial condition can compound into a monster problem over time. Think about cancer cells. They stay almost unnoticeable in the body for years. Then they grow into our worst nightmare in a matter of months. Regular check-ups and early discovery can be life saving.

"TO THE VICTOR BELONGS THE SPOILS" is another saying that describes systems thinking. It points out that the winner is the one receiving the rewards. Often, this reward, paves the path of the winner to win again. Let's say, the prize for winning was a million dollars. This money can buy the winner better equipment, quality food, and coaches. Systems thinkers call this phenomenon an archetype. Namely, "Success to the successful." Reinforcing feedback loops reward the victorious. And boost the likelihood that the same people will continue to win. This process eliminates most competitors. [1]

This process work on the other end of the spectrum, too. The current pandemic shed light on how vulnerable low-income families really were. They were in the majority to contract the coronavirus. Why? Because they lived month to month and couldn't afford not to work. They were often exposed to the virus, had lower quality masks, so they became sick. The tragedy is that -because of their income- their health was not built on organic, quality nutrition from Whole Foods. Thus the virus hit them even harder or longer. They were without payment for a painfully long time. They got trapped in a vicious reinforcing feedback loop that made their life harder every day.

WARREN BUFFET WISELY SAID, "Never test the depth of the river with both of your feet." This reminds us to protect ourselves from unfortunate events by diversification. Putting all of our efforts, hopes, and resources into one basket is risky. If something bad happens, we will find ourselves on shaky ground. Systems thinkers know that diversification is a crucial component of long-term stability.

TODAY'S WORLD view and its problems

When we shifted from an agricultural society to an industrial one, we began to rely more on scientific thinking and logic rather than instinctual reasoning. This shift made our lives easier. We accelerated transportation and shipping, found the cure for deadly diseases, and rallied together behind worthy causes to fight for. These improvements fixed some of our immediate problems. However, they resulted in new issues. Overpopulation-related issues and mass environmental destruction worsened over the decades.

Linear thinking doesn't explain the complex system problems that elude our efforts to find solutions. Issues like the opioid addiction epidemic, finding the cure for diseases like cancer and Alzheimer's, poverty, and rising suicide rates have not been solved despite the effort of multiple groups. Let's take drug abuse as an example. Interventionists and drug recovery leaders, scientists in the cutting edge of medical research, training groups helping families get out of generational poverty, and proper legislative changes are all needed to curb this problem. Their joint work is essential to address each life area where drug addiction is present. Just because you try to fix the problem in one field, it will still persist in other fields. Say, in town Z, there is a free rehabilitation center for people with drug problems. John, a long-time heroin user, decides that he had enough and joins the program. He spends three months there and recovers. But when he goes home, he finds his mom passed out after using heroin. The area where John lives is still filled with dealers keen on getting their old customer back. Before he knows it, John falls back to his old vice. The intention behind a free rehabilitation clinic is noble but it is insufficient to solve the bigger problem. Drug abuse is embedded in many layers of a large problem.

Making most drugs illegal was a quick fix to the drug problem on the political level. But it caused a lot of unintended consequences. Let's take drug-related violence as an example. Banning drugs forces dealers to sell drugs illegally, in secret. It "helped" organized crime to become more cunning and smart. And the price of the drugs increased. The users now have to pay higher costs for the products. This often means they will spend their last buck on drugs. While we can say that politically the drug question was handled, the problem itself didn't disappear following new laws and policies. Are politicians and lawmakers to blame in this situation? Or drug dealers? Or the users? Who is responsible for this problem? And more importantly, who will fix it?

IF I HAD the answer to these questions, I'd be a millionaire and hold speeches at UN conferences. The solution to drug addiction and drug-related violence won't be fixed by finding a scapegoat and blaming it. Policies that follow a cause-and-effect logic won't solve it either. The solution will come to light due to intuitive, empathetic listening, open communication, and problem-solving. When we find the wisdom and guts to restructure the system itself, we will undo the harm system structure deficits produced.

If we only do what we have always done, we will continue to get the same results we have always gotten. As Albert Einstein said, "We cannot solve our problems with the same thinking we used when we created them."

We have to the blame game and wait for an outside source to improve our situation. We need to engage in systems thinking so we can get to the root of the problem, looking at both our part in the process and the system as a whole. Each of us can contribute positively. Together we can craft real solutions. We can create the change we wish to see in the world.

THE BLIND MEN and the elephant

You may have heard of the ancient Indian fable about the blind men and the elephant. The story is about a group of blind men who encountered an elephant for the first time. Each man touches one part of the elephant; the ears, legs, trunk, and tusk. They try to understand what is in front of them. They create a picture in their minds. No two men touched the same part. When the blind men try to tell each other what they have felt, their descriptions vastly differ. They could not understand why others had such a different narrative. They assumed that the other men must either be wrong or lying.

This story teaches us an essential lesson about systems thinking: it is impossible to understand a system if we focus on its elements in isolation. To get the full story, we need to see systems as a whole and study the interactions and interdependence of its parts.

Are you ready to learn more?

Quick Systems Overview

hat is a system?

A system is a group of interconnected elements that work together to achieve a common purpose or function. To consider something a system, we need to have three things:

1. Elements;

2. Interconnections;

3. Purpose or function.

IF EVEN ONE of the above is missing, we don't have a system.

For example, our skeletal system is composed of the following elements: bones, joints, ligaments, tendons, and cartilage. These are all interconnected. The skeletal system has a vital purpose; providing a framework and support our body. Beyond that, it works with our muscular system to help our bodies move. It makes blood cells for the body, and protects our organs and soft tissues. Without these functions, we wouldn't be able to survive.

BY DEFINITION, it may seem like absolutely everything is a system, but this isn't the case. I recently stopped at a gas station located across the street from a gravel pit. As I filled up my car, I watched as large trucks came in, carrying rocks or hauling them away. The number of stones varied with each load that entered or left. But as far as the rock quarry, the rocks weren't interconnected with one another. They weren't working toward achieving a common purpose, just sitting piled up at a gravel pit. They were not a system.

SYSTEMS CAN REACT to the environment around them. They respond to changes and find ways to survive when things go wrong. This is true whether it is a living or nonliving system.

THE PARTS OF A SYSTEM:

THE ELEMENTS

These are the individual parts of the system and are usually the easiest to identify. We can see and touch them in most cases. A rose has petals, stems, roots, leaves, and thorns as elements. But they can also be intangible. For example, work morale. The elements of a family are the individual family members. Intangible elements are love, loyalty, a sense of belonging, and pride.

THE INTERCONNECTIONS

The elements work together and are linked by inter-connections. In our example of the rose system, the stem provides the flower with support. It transfers nutrients and water throughout the plant. The roots supply the flower with water. The petals attract the pollinators to foster reproduction. The thorns offer protection from predators. All of these interconnections help the rose survive.

SOMETIMES INTERCONNECTIONS ARE NOT AS easy to spot because they are not visible. Information flow is an interconnection. When we are looking closely at a system we can see these information flows occurring. For example, when a teacher evaluates a student, there is an information flow between the two elements of the evaluation system: the teacher and the student. The teacher listens closely and, based on how well the student knows the material, decides the fitting grade.

To observe hidden interconnections, you can think back to the family system. Children in a family may make decisions based on sibling rivalry or how they believe a parent will react. For example, based on their relationship with each parent, a child is likely to go to one parent over another when they want to ask for money or share the news that they received a bad grade. They will go to the more patient and knowledgeable parent to ask for help with homework. Children may decide where they would like to go to college based on where their siblings went or whether they want to be closer to or more independent from their parents.

A GOVERNMENT CAN'T MAKE good policy changes without information and research on the problematic subject. Just because they know there is a problem doesn't mean they can take productive action without having the necessary data, research, and listening to the voices of the relevant constituents. Without enough information, making a decision is just as safe as relying on blindfolded, dart-throwing monkeys to hit the center of the dartboard. And since bad political decisions are likely to cost a politician's seat in office, they are likely to have all the research and data needed before changing any policies.

IN A SYSTEM, just knowing about a problem's existence isn't enough to lead to an informed decision. You also need to know what positive outcomes the change may create. What types of consequences may accompany the decision? What help or information is available? The deeper the understanding of the subject, the better the chances of reaching the desired outcome.

. . .

FUNCTION OR PURPOSE

WHEN IT COMES TO SYSTEMS, the word function is usually used to describe nonhuman systems. Purpose is used when discussing human systems. The denomination can be mixed, though, since many systems are made of both human and nonhuman elements.

THE FUNCTION or purpose of a system isn't always clearly spelled out in the same way that a mission statement or goals or objectives might be for a company. Often, the best way to really know the purpose of a system is to observe it in action and watch its behavior over time.

"ACTIONS SPEAK LOUDER THAN WORDS." This saying stands true when determining the purpose of a system. An example of actions versus words would be a politician who makes many campaign promises about their purpose while running for office. But it will be their behavior displayed and promises kept once in office that reveals their real purpose.

THE FUNCTION of almost every system is the will and work to ensure its own survival. Think back to the rose system. The petals have the job of attracting pollinators to the plant to reproduce and ensure that there will be more roses in the future. Simultaneously, the thorns on a rose serve to protect it so that the rose system wards off predators. In our example of the politician, they must make campaign promises to attract financial contributors and voters to ensure success in a primary.

IT CAN ALSO HAPPEN that the system's real purpose ends up being something that was not wanted by any of the elements. Think about the war on drugs. It is also possible for systems to have more than one purpose at the same time. Or for the elements within the system to be working toward different purposes. Let's look at the example of high-stakes standardized testing in public schools to demonstrate how this can happen. I will list some of the elements at play and their intended individual purposes:

. . .

•POLITICIANS WANT to demonstrate to their constituents that they are invested in the education of public school children.

•PARENTS WANT their children to be academically successful and achieve high test scores.

•SCHOOL DISTRICTS WANT to receive higher scores to be competitive with other nearby districts and attract more students, better teachers, – and more federal and state funds.

•TEACHERS WANT their students to do well as a means of job security, and in some cases, to earn merit pay.

•STUDENTS WANT to do well and avoid being retained in a grade or taking remedial or summer school classes. They want to avoid parental disappointment and social ridicule.

. . .

•COMPANIES WHO SELL educational materials want to make money by writing high-stakes tests, providing practice or remedial materials, creating software programs and technology, writing textbooks, and providing staff development programs for teachers. They develop measures for students that test for autism, learning disabilities, emotional disturbance, etc.

THE GENUINE EFFORT TO ensure that students were being taught the curriculum assigned to them and received extra help if they weren't meeting certain benchmarks quickly turned into a dysfunctional system of pressure, money poorly spent, and chronic teacher burnout. The original purpose was weighed down and obliterated by all the sub-purposes competing within the larger system. The elements became so concerned about their own individual goals that the unifying purpose got lost.

TODAY, high stakes, standardized testing is controversial. Students are experiencing anxiety over testing, not to mention that the tests' measures are rarely perfect indicators of potential or ability. Many parents and teachers are alarmed by the amount of school time being spent teaching to the test and how much of the district's budget is spent on testing materials. Some parents are opting out of having their children take the tests altogether.

TEACHING HAS BECOME MORE competitive and less cooperative. Teachers are trying to outperform each other to ensure job security and merit pay rather than supporting fellow teachers and helping students who are academically at risk. Many have left the profession and fewer professionals choose to enter it right out of college, creating a teacher shortage. [1]

LOW-PERFORMING schools are penalized by having their state funds taken away. When these are the schools that need it the most. As a result, well-performing teachers leave the school in frustration seeking better opportunities. Thereby they are leaving the schools that have the most minorities, learning disabled, or economically disadvantaged students who'd need well-trained educators the most. [2] [3]

· · ·

THE SUB-SYSTEMS and sub-purposes within the larger system began to work against one another. The result was a system no longer delivering its original purpose: having well-educated and happy children. The system has instead created negative consequences that no one ever wanted or intended.

THE SUB-PURPOSES and the main purpose of a system have to be kept in harmony. Later in this book, we'll see examples of how we can bring people with different sub-purposes to the table and work toward a compromised agreement.

WHAT CHANGES A SYSTEM THE MOST?

USUALLY, changing the elements has the smallest impact on the system. In the school system example, exchanging the teachers, staff, administrators, and students with new ones, we could still recognize the system as a school.

CHANGING the interconnections has a more significant impact on the system as a whole. Even if we didn't change any element, changing some interconnections could alter the system to the point of being unrecognizable. If a public school was changed to a private school where students were required to pay tuition to attend, the system would differ. Students might not worry about standardized tests that have strict measures, and they might have their pick of the best teachers. The teachers might be religiously affiliated and be required to adhere to a rigorous code of conduct.

SOME PRIVATE SCHOOLS might also lack diversity, as lower SES students are more like to be people of color. [4] A school in Louisiana had a policy against hair extensions specifically targeting to exclude black girls from the school. This policy has been deemed racist and rescinded in August 2018. [5]

CHANGING the purpose or function of a system can produce even more drastic results. What if a school's purpose was no longer to educate students but to only cater to them while their parents are working? Or if only those children who specifically ask for it would be educated?

ALL COMPONENTS WITHIN A SYSTEM: elements, interconnections, and function or purpose are equally important to the success of the system. They all have their jobs to do. Ironically, the part of the system that is the hardest to recognize, the function or purpose, has the most significant influence on the system's behavior. The most easily recognizable parts – the elements – often play the smallest role in determining a system's behavior. But this isn't always the case. In the school system example, changing the headmaster might greatly impact defining the system if the switch also changed the purpose or interconnections. Just think of how much Hogwarts changed after Dolores Umbridge replaced Albus Dumbledore…

STOCKS AND FLOWS

STOCKS ARE the building blocks of any system. They are the measurable elements. In the school system example, the stocks would be:

- the number of students,

- the test scores,

- the amount of time or money spent on testing,

- the number of textbooks available for different subjects,

- the stress and anxiety levels of the students and teachers,

- and the number of voters who supported a politician's position on education.

THESE ARE all examples of stocks. Stocks can be living beings, inanimate objects, or conceptual things.

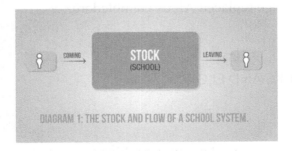

DIAGRAM 1: THE STOCK AND FLOW OF A SCHOOL SYSTEM.

DIAGRAM 1: Stock and Flow

Stocks change over time based on the flows. In a school system, flows are students who move in or out of a district. The number of students in schools depends on the birth rate, demographics, and ages of the people living in the community. The amount of money going into the district is dependent on the tax rates approved by the legislature and voters. The test scores depend on student performance, the way the questions are asked. These are all flows that impact and change the system. Stocks act as a current snapshot of the changing actions of the flows in a system.

ON DIAGRAM 1, you can see how stocks and flows work. The big rectangle in the middle is the stock itself, in our case, the school. There is an inflow affecting the stock, the arriving students. The stock also has an outflow: students who leave, graduate, or drop out. The inflow and outflow affecting the school stock could be other things: the inflow and outflow of school funds, the average success of the students taking tests, the teacher's motivation after changes in salary.

. . .

UNDERSTANDING the dynamics of stocks and flows and their behaviors over time can help you see the system's behavior as a whole.

SOME SYSTEMS DON'T HAVE inflow. Let's look at the example of a newly found oil field. It took Mother Nature hundreds of thousands of years to create the oil reservoir under the ground. We can safely bet that if someone starts extracting the oil from this field, he will do it quicker than nature can replace it.

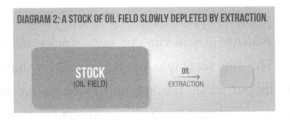

DIAGRAM 2: A STOCK OF OIL FIELD SLOWLY DEPLETED BY EXTRACTION.

STOCK
(OIL FIELD)

OIL
EXTRACTION

Diagram 2: Stock with one outflow.

UNDERSTANDING Graphs

SYSTEMS THINKERS ARE MORE interested in studying trends over time than individual events.

They use graphs to help make these trends visual. When looking at a graph that displays a system's behavior over time, they can see if a system is close to reaching a goal or a limit and how quickly it might get there. The variable on the graph is often a stock or flow.

WHEN YOU LOOK at a graph through a systems thinking lens, you want to be less concerned with exact numbers on the graph. They represent a snapshot of just a moment in time and individual events. It better serves you to look at the shape of the variable line and the places where the line changes shape or direction. Those are the representations of the trends and behaviors over time. The horizontal axis shows you the timeline of the trends happening in the system. You can see what happened before and forecast what might come next.

IF YOU HAVE EVER LIVED with children, you know that they can accumulate quite the collection of toys. For the purpose of this example, picture a child having fifty toys. If you stop buying new toys for the child and keep the toys she currently has, there will be no inflow or outflow. The number of toys the child has will stay the same. This represents a stagnant system.

SUPPOSE you no longer purchase new toys, and the child continuously breaks the existing ones. In that case, the collection will drop in number until eventually there aren't any toys left. (See Diagram 3.) In other words, the stock only has one outflow. Let's say the child breaks five toys weekly. You can follow the trend of the decreasing stock by reviewing the graph of your child's behavior. Imagine you are in week four. By then, the child broke twenty toys. Considering that originally there are fifty toys, the total stock of the toys will be depleted in ten weeks.

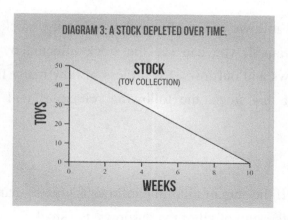

DIAGRAM 3: A stock depleted over time.

BUT WHAT IF the child breaks one toy at the same speed as she receives a new one. What will happen to the toy collection now? The number of toys will stay constant at the current number because the inflow of new toys is now equal to the outflow of the old toys. One comes, one goes. The stock is now in a state of dynamic equilibrium. The stock level (toys) doesn't change even though there are continuous inflows and outflows in the system.

THE TOY COLLECTION example represented a straightforward system where there was only one stock, one inflow, and one outflow. There can be more inflows and outflows that affect the stock. On Diagram 4, you can see the stock affected by two inflows and outflows. Regardless of how many flows affect this stock, the following principles will hold true:

- If the sum of all of the inflows is greater than the sum of all of the outflows, the stock amount will increase.
- If the sum of all of the outflows is greater than the sum of all of the inflows, the stock amount will decrease.
- If the sum of all of the inflows and the sum of all of the outflows are equal, the stock amount will not change. It will remain in a state of dynamic equilibrium at the level when the inflows and outflows became equal.

DIAGRAM 4: A STOCK WITH MORE INFLOWS AND OUTFLOWS.

GIFTED TOYS

SELF-MADE TOYS

STOCK
(TOYS IN THE HOUSEHOLD)

BROKEN TOYS

DONATED TOYS

DIAGRAM 4: A stock with multiple inflows and outflows.

OUR BRAIN MAKES common mistakes when it comes to stocks and flows. It is human nature to think more about stocks than flows. In the example of our bank account, we pay more attention to the total amount of money we currently have than we do to our income or spending. When we pay attention to flows, it is more natural for us to focus on the inflow rather than the outflow. If we are not accumulating the amount of wealth that we want to, we are more likely to want more income, than to decrease our expenses.

We can change the flows of our systems quicker than the level of our stock. We can immediately start to increase our income by taking a second job, or decreasing our spending by eating out less. But it will take some time to see the results reflected on our bank balance.

It takes time for stocks to change because it takes time for flows to flow. Stocks change more slowly (especially if they are large) because they react to change gradually. Delays between the change of the flow and the stock's response impact the system. It takes a long time to populate virgin soil with a forest. Even with the right incentives, years will pass until a country's population shows growth or decay.

The delays and gaps in time before stocks react to change can cause problems for systems, but they can also serve as a stabilizing factor. For example, the more machines evolve, the more human workplaces they claim. However, these changes don't get implemented immediately. There is a delay when replacing human labor with a machine. The worker can mentally prepare for the change, find a new job, or learn a new skill. Delays can also buy us time to observe and reflect on what is happening in the system. We can make changes before major damage has been done.

But you can approach the example of machines replacing humans from a different angle. Think of Charlie and the Chocolate Factory, where Mr. Bucket had a miserable job putting the lids on toothpaste containers. At some point, his position became automated by a machine. He got a better job - fixing the machine that had replaced him. He got paid a better wage because it was a more skilled position...

The existence of stocks makes it possible for flows to act independently of one another and to be out of balance in the short term. The fact that you have savings in your account makes it possible for your spending to be larger than your income for a limited period.

We make most of our individual and system decisions because we want to control our stock level. If I run out of peppermint tea, it isn't long before I head to the store to buy more. If the gas in my tank starts running low, I begin to look for the nearest gas station.

The decisions you make and actions you take are made to keep your stock level within an acceptable range. You can control the levels of these stocks by adjusting the flows in the system. How can you adjust the flows? By utilizing "feedback processes."

Feedback Loops

Regardless of whether a stock level rises, drops, or remains constant, we can conclude that there is a control mechanism in place to maintain either of these behaviors. Control mechanisms work through feedback loops.

A feedback loop happens when changes in the stock impact the inflows and outflows. For example, the amount of money in your bank account (stock) impacts how much interest you earn. The more money you have in your account, the more interest you will gain. If the amount of money you have in the bank (stock) drops, you will earn less interest. This is an example of a simple feedback loop where the change in the stock affects its flows. [6]

Balancing Feedback Loops

I have a friend who was diagnosed as being pre-diabetic. It was a warning sign. He had to keep an eye on his sugar intake and change other habits to prevent advancing to full-blown diabetes. There were times during the day when his hands started shaking, and he felt light-headed. This was a sign of his blood sugar level dropping too low. He had to eat some food to stabilize it. He knew how his body felt when his insulin level was within the normal range. He took action based on the feedback he got from his body. The stock of blood sugar was fluctuating based on the flow of simple carbohydrates converted to glucose during digestion. (See Diagram 5, where B stands for balancing feedback loop.)

Diagram 5: A stock and a balancing feedback.

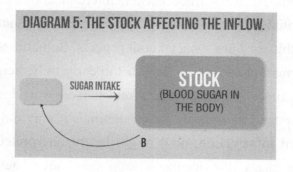

Balancing feedback loops seek stability and always have the goal of keeping stock levels within the range deemed acceptable. If a stock level is too high, the balancing feedback loop will work to bring it back down where it should be and vice versa.

Just because a feedback mechanism exists doesn't mean it's functioning well. Sometimes it isn't strong enough to overcome significant increases or decreases in stocks to return them to optimal levels. For example, suppose the inflation is 3%, and your savings account offers 2% interest. In that case, your purchasing power will decrease despite trying to balance inflation-related loss with your interest-earning account.

The feedbacks stand for the interconnections in the system. As we learned earlier, interconnections hold essential information that a system needs to function. But this isn't always a smooth process. Sometimes the information arrives too late or too early to be helpful. Sometimes it goes to the wrong person who doesn't understand its importance. Sometimes it may only be partial information, or it might be misinterpreted. In some cases, the feedback loop may never get the stock to reach its target.

Reinforcing Feedback Loops

The other type of feedback loop is the reinforcing one. This loop magnifies and multiplies results, creating a cycle that can be hard to break free from. It can cause exceptional growth or decline.

Reinforcing feedback loops are at work when the rich get richer, and the poor get poorer. When people have a lot of money or an excellent credit score, they can borrow money at the lowest interest rates. Then they can reinvest it to make even more money. When people have a lower credit score and less money, they are forced to pay higher interest rates on their debt. Thus, income inequity between the upper, middle, and lower classes continues to widen.

Reinforcing feedback loops magnify whatever change, causing the increases or decreases to be more significant over time.

Here are a few examples:

- When animals become endangered, there are fewer adults left to produce offspring. This means that the numbers can't grow at the required rate to remove them from the endangered species list.
- When people earn more money, they make more purchases. When people are purchasing more goods, the demand is high, and the supply is low. This causes merchants to be able to charge more for their products. As a result, people need to continue to earn more to purchase goods at the same rate.
- The more rain falls, the more standing water there is. The standing water is a breeding ground for mosquitos. As a result, the mosquitos can reproduce at more rapid rates.
- When child A calls child B names, child B typically responds by calling names in return. The negative exchange can escalate and

continue between the children until someone steps in to intervene.

- When an athlete practices, they become more skilled in their sport. When they are better at their sport, they tend to enjoy it more. One naturally enjoys activities they are already good at. The athlete wants to spend more time with their sport, leading to more practice and further skill improvement.

Reinforcing feedback loops are self-supporting and can multiply rapidly. These loops exist anytime a stock can adjust its own level. Diagram 6 presents the reinforcing feedback loop (where R stands for reinforcing feedback) of reproducing rabbits in places where their natural predators decreased. The more rabbits survive, the more offspring they will have. If there is no human intervention and no increase in predators, the barrier to their growth would be the food available and the fighting between the male rabbits in the warren. But right now, let's just focus on the variables presented in the diagram.

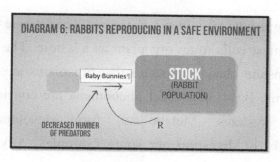

DIAGRAM 6: RABBITS REPRODUCING IN A SAFE ENVIRONMENT

Baby Bunnies

STOCK
(RABBIT POPULATION)

DECREASED NUMBER
OF PREDATORS

R

Diagram 6: A stock and a reinforcing feedback.

What feedback loops can you encounter in your daily life? If you can think of any, you are well on your way to becoming a systems thinker. When you think in systems, you don't for scapegoats. You want to understand and examine why certain things happen.

You see that the behaviors and interconnections of a system, over time, can lead to different outcomes than expected. For example, you can notice that not only X has an impact on Y, but also Y can reflect back on X through a feedback mechanism.

Before we learn about how we can use systems thinking in practice, let's differentiate between two types of systems: open and closed systems.

OPEN AND CLOSED **systems**

Living things are always changing. This is true from the tiniest cells to an organism as a whole. The state of constant change indicates that organisms are open systems. Basic biological phenomena are considered open systems. Metabolism, form development, growth, or digestion are some examples. Anything that has a cell and therefore relies on osmosis.

In an open system, materials are entering and leaving. The inflow and outflow of materials serve to perpetually change the system because its individual elements are also continually being changed.

In a closed system, interactions only happen within the system. No material is entering or leaving. We can say closed systems are shut off from the outside environment. This type of system has set processes that are not affected by external stimuli. A closed system exchanges energy only with its surroundings. Putting strawberries in a freezer is a closed system because freezers are airtight. Matter can no longer transfer. The door prevents matter from entering and leaving the freezer. When variations in time disappear, the closed systems become stationary. They attain a state of equilibrium where the system composition remains constant. Closed systems must eventually reach a state of equilibrium, according to the second law of thermodynamics. [78]

Open systems can also attain a state of equilibrium. The trick for this is for the inflow and outflow to be at the same rate.

4

Mental Models

D o you remember the model of the solar system you saw in astronomy books? Or the model of an airplane or a car you built as a hobby? Or a computer simulation that shows a model of something complicated you use at work? You have been exposed to models before.

What are models in systems thinking? Models take a complex system and simplify it, making it easier to understand. They are the abstract or simplified representation of something larger.

Are models the perfect mirror of what they aim to represent? No. Models show only a part of the system we want to analyze. They crop a piece of reality out of the whole to help us study it closely and learn from it. When creating a model, we don't add every variable and influencing factor of a situation on purpose. Taking every aspect into consideration would not make a complicated matter digestible. Thus, models are - and should - never be the final reality, but rather a tool that gets us closer to seeing and understanding a complex system's real objective. Models are helpful learning tools.

Mental models are created within the mind. They are cognitive tools. To create a useful mental model, you need to know how your mind works and how you download information from your brain into your model. What do I mean by this?

Imagine that you walk out in your backyard and see a rabbit sitting there. What happens? Your eyes receive the image of the rabbit and send messages about it to your brain. In the initial split second that you see the rabbit, you don't know what you're actually seeing. You're just receiving visual information. It isn't until the visual information reaches your brain that the understanding of the rabbit deepens. The rabbit is a concept of your external reality. But you wouldn't understand what you're seeing is a rabbit if you've never seen a rabbit before or you didn't know what a rabbit looks like.

The information from your eyes and other sensory organs is not enough to create understanding. Part of what it takes to acknowledge what the rabbit is, as a concept, comes from past experiences and prior knowledge. Your experience surrounding the idea of the fluffy carrot muncher creates your mental model about it.

If you know the same rabbits I do, we can agree that the rabbit is a mammal known for its strong sense of hearing and quickness, which helps it escape from predators. Depending on the type of rabbit and where it lives, its fur color may change with the seasons to help it use camouflage and blend in more with its surroundings for protection. It is an herbivore, which means it eats plants. It breathes in oxygen and exhales carbon dioxide. Thanks to the mental model I have in my brain about rabbits, I can be confident that rabbits won't attack me, and I need not be alarmed or fearful when looking at them. I can conclude that I'm safe if a rabbit is in my backyard. I state this with a strong belief based on my past experiences with and prior knowledge of rabbits.

Mental models are designed of knowledge that we already have, and they help us add new knowledge or deepen understanding.

In a simple system model, like a causal loop diagram, a cause and effect relationship links the elements in action. Sometimes, however, we can't immediately see the thought processes behind these connections. How does investing in leadership development result in less employee turnover? How can a change in communication style lead to an improved relationship? How does a gesture of kindness change the opinion of our rivals?

Understanding the mental models behind these cause and effect connections helps to acknowledge the mechanisms responsible for creating certain behaviors. It can also allow us to come up with better solutions to problems.

To map out our mental models based on our thought processes, we create causal loop diagrams. Putting our observations in a visual form helps us go beyond superficial understanding. We will be able to see things and find connections that we would miss otherwise. We call this step going deeper.

How do we "go deeper?"

We design a causal loop diagram for a system-level problem. (See an example of a causal loop diagram in Diagram 7.)

We look at our completed diagram and search for links that result from human decisions. For example, a headline such as "the change in state support negatively affected the budget for health care" is a mathematical reality. The less money an institution receives, the less it will have to distribute. If we look at the decision-makers behind the new health care policies, we can see human involvement.

When we find a connection point due to human choice, we need to ask this question: Why is this decision made?

Try to get into the mindset and perspective of the decision-makers. Once you feel like you understand their viewpoint, add it to the map by drawing a thought bubble above the human choice connection.

TYPES OF MENTAL **Models**

PREDICTIONS AND GUESSES

When we use mental models, our minds are automatically jumping to conclusions about what will come next. Let's play a game. Imagine a dog jumping for a ball. What are your thoughts on this picture? Did you just imagine the dog catching the ball? Or you imagined it missing the ball and falling back to the ground while the ball rolls away?

REGARDLESS OF WHAT YOU IMAGINED, you were unconsciously using your mental models. You can't know what happens next in a static picture. Thus your imagination is a prediction or a guess. Multiple conclusion scenarios are possible. Using mental models primes your brain to think about possible future outcomes and consequences.

THE THEORY **of Constraints**[1]

If you've ever heard the phrase "a team is only as strong as its weakest link," then you have an understanding of this type of mental model. The Theory of Constraints recognizes that every system is limited. By nature, there will always be one constraint that exerts more pressure on a system than others. This becomes the bottleneck that causes the biggest problem in the system. [2]

. . .

A SYSTEM CAN ONLY PERFORM AS WELL as its weakest link. Therefore, a bottleneck issue will negatively impact the performance of the entire system, which will only improve once the bottleneck is resolved.

WE CAN TAKE this idea to our own personal improvement goals. If we don't figure out the real source of what is holding us back from living the life we deserve - our bottleneck problem - we will continue to run in circles. We may make some changes and even feel like we are moving forward, but we will not get where we want if the bottleneck isn't addressed. We don't need to work harder, just smarter. We need to find the area of maximum impact. For example, if we have anger issues due to childhood neglect, we will not be better off learning nonviolent communication. We will only shout prettier words. Once we address the whys and hows of our childhood stories and re-learn our coping mechanisms, we can focus on healthy communication tips.

REMOVING a bottleneck is not the end of our journey. We will always be a work in progress. Once we clear our current bottleneck, we move on to the next. When we overcome a bottleneck issue, the entire system will go through a changing phase; it will readjust to the new circumstances.

USE mental models to identify bottlenecks. Remember, first design a causal loop diagram, and then identify human decisions among the links. Ask, "Why is this decision made?" Answer it. Then analyze if this decision is prolonging, triggering, or reinforcing the existence of the problem. Dig deeper if you've confirmed that the decision is a possible catalyst for the problem. How? By trying to find the trigger. I know, I'm spiraling out of the easy-to-follow framework. I will present how to use mental models to identify bottlenecks with the example of trying to lose weight.

LET'S imagine Jack who wants to lose 20 pounds. He works out for two hours five times a week. But after each gruesome spinning session, he goes straight to Lazy Acres buying those delicious chocolate chip cookies. Despite pushing his limits and depleting his willpower, he doesn't experience significant weight loss. The human decision, in this case, is eating calorie-rich, nutrition-lacking snacks.

"WHY DID HE MAKE THIS DECISION?" Because Jack has eaten all his life mindlessly. Research studies have shown that sugar is more addicting in lab rats than crack. I swear, those Lazy Acres chocolate chip cookies have them both. Perhaps Jack rationalizes that because he just burned 700 calories in the gym, he can now eat whatever he wants. This is not how diets work. And he knows it. Why doesn't he respect the effort he put into his goal at the gym? This is a great question.

THE LACK of self-control and the purposeful self-sabotage can be rooted in low self-respect and a lack of self-love. Jack doesn't consider himself worthy of his goals. He has a negative self-image and bad habits.

WHILE AT THE beginning of the analysis, it may have seemed that binging was the bottleneck problem of this man. After digging deeper, we've discovered that low self-esteem is the real cause of the unsuccessful diet. Self-sabotage is just another symptom of a more profound problem.

IF JACK GAVE up on the cookies and achieved his target weight, he'd probably still be unhappy. He didn't fix his bottleneck problem. He would find another "imperfection" to torment himself with.

WITH THE HELP of a mental model (and a good therapist), Jack could identify his bottleneck problem and work towards dissolving it. If he became more accepting and kind to himself, he would want to nurture his body and stay healthy. He would stick to his diet for the same reason. Thus, he'd reach his goal of weight loss and also satisfaction.

Feedback Loop Installation[3]

We discussed feedback loops in the last chapter. We have balancing feedback loops that work to maintain equilibrium. And reinforcing feedback loops which can either cause growth or decline in a system.

. . .

PEOPLE IMPLANT BALANCING feedback loops in systems when they want to keep it steady and consistent. They protect themselves from unforeseeable events rocking the boat. These pre-implanted balancing feedback loops are checkpoints that can reduce the damage of an adverse event. They give people time and opportunity for reflection to decide the next best step.

WE NEED to stay aware of the counterbalancing feedback loops around us as well. What goes around comes back around, the saying goes. Sometimes a balancing feedback loop, originally meant to balance the system, overflows. To keep the equilibrium, some other forces start to take action. For example, we want to save $100 every month. Suppose we start spending more on hobbies to enhance our life quality. In that case, we'll need to cut spending in other areas, like our essentials Or we can aim to earn more so we need to work overtime or take a second, part-time job. To balance the loop of hobbies, the counterbalancing loop of cutting expenses on essentials or working overtime steps in (assuming that we'll stick to our $100 saving plan no matter what).

PUT this idea on a larger scale. The government needs to maintain a state budget that can't decrease under a certain level. Otherwise, the state will go bankrupt. Usually, there would be a mandatory percentage budget cut, and all state agencies would have to do them. But if this rectification is not enough and they don't want to raise taxes, they need to tighten their belts in other areas. The government will cut funds from education, health, or research and development. Conversely, suppose the government wishes to dispense more money to R&D and education. In that case, it needs to collect more in taxes to keep the fragile balance of the state budget.

REINFORCING feedback loops are implanted when we want to continually set higher standards for our system and assure growth over time. If we're going to achieve long-lasting growth, we have to start with small steps.

. . .

FOR EXAMPLE, the $100 savings we invest in a low-risk stock will grow exponentially over time.

THE BORROWING EXAMPLE

We can create mental models of things that are tangible, simple, and recent more easily. The process becomes more challenging when the things we analyze are abstract or removed from our personal experience. Let's take a closer look at the example of borrowing money.

A YOUNG COUPLE had to make unforeseeable purchases on their credit card. They were short on cash. Over time, the credit card's high interest rate caused an even bigger financial problem. To create a mental model that gives insight into the couple's situation, follow these five steps: [4]

1.DRAW A CAUSAL LOOP DIAGRAM:

Borrowing money seemed like a good solution to the shortage of readily available funds. When you borrow money, you have access to more cash, but this will only help in the short-term. (B1 – As you borrow money, the cash shortage temporarily decreases.) As time goes on, high interest payments will reduce the amount of money you have. (R1) This solution ultimately proves to be unsuccessful.

2.ADD A THOUGHT BUBBLE to any link where a human choice was involved.

The human choice in this example the decision to borrow money. Add this choice to the arrow connecting "Cash Flow Problems" and "Borrowing."

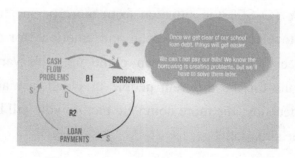

Diagram 7: The case of borrowing[5]

3.ASSUME THE BORROWER THINKS RATIONALLY. Ask yourself, "why did the couple make the decision to borrow and then borrow even more to cover the expense of his first borrowing?"

4.TRY TO COME up with several explanations. Perhaps they were worried about "keeping up with the Joneses" and needed money for appearances. Or maybe they felt cornered; they saw no other choice than to borrow money to provide for their family and pay their bills. Maybe they planned to borrow money to get through a rough financial patch and thought their life circumstances would improve soon.

5.TRY TO SEE the situation from more perspectives. Try to understand the reason and emotions for their choice. The more you can come up with various reasons for the different people involved in making the decision, the more complete picture you will have of the situation. [6]

BY GOING DEEPER, we learn a lot about the system and why it behaves the way it does. If we only looked at the system's superficial aspects, we would miss out on the hidden reasons that come with a more profound analysis. Jumping to conclusions and finding someone to blame for problems within the system, we wouldn't learn valuable information on the bottleneck issue and couldn't fix it.

GOING EVEN DEEPER

Our ultimate goal is to use our deeper understanding to take action and change the system for the better.

WE HAVE DISCUSSED MAKING causal loop diagrams using mental models. But Richard Karash and Michael Goodman take this process a few steps further, as explained in their article Going Deeper: Moving from Understanding to Action. [7] Here are the next four steps they advise aspiring systems thinkers to take into consideration:

1.EXPLORE THE PURPOSE

Ask yourself where you are now and where you hope to be. Take a hard, honest look at your current reality. Where are you at the present time? How would a successful outcome for the system look like? Only by knowing all these answers can you begin to close the gap and achieve your vision.

2.EXAMINE MENTAL MODELS

Go deeper than the superficial layer of a system. Assume that everyone involved is acting rationally. Try to understand why they made the decisions they did. These ideas should get added to the causal loop diagrams as thought bubbles.

3.ACKNOWLEDGE PERSONAL RESPONSIBILITY

It is human nature to want to place blame outside of ourselves when things go wrong. That's how we're wired. The problem with that line of thinking, though, is that it also gives away our power. If we refuse to accept the role we might play in the current problems of the system, we give away our ability to be a part of a real and lasting solution. Systems thinkers don't blame; they look for solutions. Often a positive change begins with us.

4.EXPAND THE VIEW

Problems in systems rarely occur in a vacuum. They have connections to both the past and the future. We just have to be willing to look for them. Has the system ever been in the same situation before? What is your vision for future success? Learning from the past and creating a bridge to the future is vital in improving a system. Consider all possible consequences before making an action plan. Then start moving forward.

5

Systems Essentials

All high-functioning systems have three characteristics in common: they are resilient, self-organizing, or a thriving hierarchy.

RESILIENCE

Systems are pushed and stretched - often to their limits. Their long-term success is measured by their ability to bounce back and recover on time from challenges and adversity. Adaptability and elasticity are the keywords. Various feedback loops help the system recover when it strays off its path and away from achieving its purpose or function.

. . .

RESILIENCE ISN'T easy to recognize, especially if we don't look at the system as a whole. For example, if we examined a broken bone within the first three days of breaking, we might conclude that the human body is not resilient. If, however, we looked at the same broken bone a year later, we saw how resilient our body really is. When we look at the system's behavior over time, we can really confirm its resilience.

THERE ARE cases when systems lose their resilience. Take your own body, for example. It is exposed to many viruses and bacteria each day without you being aware of it. If your immune system is robust, it will fight back against the invaders and stay healthy. You might catch a cold depending on the germ, but you'll heal eventually. But resilience can be lost with aging. This is especially true in the case of living systems. Think about bone density depletion over a woman's lifetime. Due to the brittleness of her bones, the hip breaks easier if she falls. Then, because of the same brittleness, the recovery is longer. Her health declines because she doesn't exercise regularly or eat as well.

Standing to cook is a strain. This woman would need an orthopedist and a skilled internist who would look at her nutritional health, a physical therapist, and a therapist to help her mental health. An injury like this could devastate an otherwise vibrant person. It is a profound breakdown of multiple subsystems in her body.

SOME DISASTERS HAPPEN because of human involvement. Ford Motor Company and its dumping of toxic sludge on or near lands for the Ramapough Mountain Indians contaminated the community's soil, air, and groundwater for a long time. The Ramapough Mountain Tribe and other residents of Ringwood, New Jersey, sued Ford Motor Company for property damage. (Wayne Mann, et al. v. Ford Motor Company, et al. case) [1]

DUE to rapidly changing weather conditions caused by wastewater treatment ponds and the smokestacks from the Bowater Paper Mill, there was a 100 car pileup on a three-mile stretch of I-75 in Tennessee. This resulted in thirteen fatalities and forty-two injuries.

This stretch of road was already notoriously dangerous for sudden, blindingly thick fog. After this accident, the Tennessee Department of Transportation implemented more measures to help drivers see and closing access to the highway once fog reached a specific density. Still, even Bowater's own report analysts stated that the smokestacks prevented the water vapor from rising off the wastewater ponds. That was creating the deadly fog partially responsible for the accidents. [2]

SOME SPECIES GO EXTINCT due to changed environmental conditions. They lose their resilience and adaptability because the change is too extreme to withstand. Other species overpopulate because they don't have any natural predators anymore. The use of certain pesticides in the farming industry temporarily solved the problem of crop munching insects. But just as these insects disappeared, other insect populations rose to power. They were more resilient, and the old pesticides were not effective on them. Using stronger or different pesticides would not have helped in the long term either. While some species would always become dominant, the soil would get saturated with poison in the chemical war against the insects. [3]

. . .

THERE WERE attempts to break the vicious pesticide circle by introducing new, natural predators to farms. This method has been mostly unsuccessful outside of the animals' natural ecosystem. In Australia, they introduced the cane toad to prey on a specific beetle that disrupted sugar cane production. The toads did their "job" well, but they also had no natural predators. These toads are poisonous to the touch as they carry toxin in their skin. Since Australian predators aren't adapted to the toxin, they may kill the frog, but it often costs them their lives. The cane toads are prolific breeders, and all attempts to manage or curb them have failed. [4]

WE'VE SEEN similar issues in the Everglades, Florida, with two apex predators: alligators and the errantly introduced pythons. Wayward owners wanted to get rid of a constrictor that has gotten too big, expensive, and no longer wanted. Properly rehoming the animal takes time. So owners were just releasing them in masse in the wild where they are now breading uncontrollably in a hidden environment. [5]

. . .

EACH CHANGE we make in a system affects its resilience. That is why it is essential to examine and predict how a system would react to our interventions from many angles and anticipate every possible outcome and consequence before taking action.

SOME THINGS MAY SOUND APPEALING in the short-term. But we don't really want to sacrifice a system's resilience and make it more dependent on human involvement. Our ultimate goal should be to ensure that systems can persevere through adversity with as little unnatural input as possible.

YOU HAVE LIKELY HEARD the Chinese proverb, "Give a man a fish, and you feed him for a day. Teach a man to fish, and you feed him for a lifetime." This stands true in the case of systems. We want them to be able to function on their own as independently as possible. We should aim to boost a systems' self-restorative ability.

IN CASE of the pesticide-insect issue, instead of intervening chemically, natural ecosystems should be promoted. The predators of the insects we wish to get rid of should be allowed to handle the pests. Sustainable farming techniques that retain soil quality over the long-term should be practiced over methods that pillage the soil of all its riches in a few short years. This way, the balance of nature wouldn't be disturbed, and the soil quality wouldn't degrade. [6]

SELF-ORGANIZATION

ANOTHER CHARACTERISTIC OF well-functioning systems is self-organization. Think about how the first communities, tribes, city-states, and, later, nation-states evolved out of formerly scattered humans. People learned to live in communities, developed and diversified their skills. As their community became more complex, they established laws and guidelines to keep this complexity in relative order.

SELF-ORGANIZATION IS A VALUABLE ABILITY, but it is so general in living systems that we hardly take it into consideration. Unfortunately, we are often oblivious to the evolution of self-organization in front of us. We fail to aid it, or worse, we perpetually work against it.

FOR EXAMPLE, when we overdose on caffeine to stay awake despite our body being on the brink of exhaustion. We may influence our body's processes in the short-term, but this interference backfires later. If we are continuously sleep-deprived, our body system will shut down so that no amount of caffeine can resurrect it.

GIVING TOO many instructions and overly strict evaluations can kill employees' creativity and morale. Relying too much on old rules may give one a sense of control and stability, but in the long run, it banishes innovation and optimization.

SUPPORTING self-organization in a system requires a loosening of the reins. Be willing to let go of a bit of control to give the system the chance and freedom to do what comes naturally. Allow a degree of trial and error within the system. This is often difficult as things can become messy at times. It can be challenging for people to adopt a hands-off policy long enough to let self-organization work. It's like wanting to let your kids use paint and glitter for an art project but being terrified of the mess that they'll make. Sometimes we intervene because we can't help ourselves.

LUCKILY, no constraint lasts forever. Even under Cambodia's heaviest stone-built temples, trees and vegetation found a way to break to the surface. After the bloodiest wars and deadliest diseases, the nations affected have found a way to move on, re-organize themselves, adapt to the new circumstances, and rebuild. Cambodia is an excellent example of this Phoenix-like resurrection. Under the terroristic rules of the Khmer Rouge, 1.5 to 3 million people died. It was known as Cambodia's Killing Fields. [7] Some holy places were filled up with the dead bodies of innocent casualties. Yet, after the horror was over, Cambodia's people buried and properly mourned their dead, and cleansed the holy places. Today, together, in unity, they pray for a better future.

. . .

NOT ALL NATIONS thrive after a difficult period. Free nations usually thrive, but very corrupt governments are often corrupt at their people's expense. The Democratic Republic of Congo is one of the world's richest countries in terms of natural resources. It has the minerals that our cell phones, computers, and gaming systems cannot be made without. They have a unique copper belt, yet many Congolese people don't have running water in their homes. [8] Child labor is a part of life there. The men are ill-equipped for the heavy-duty mining they do, often wearing cheap Wellington boots-like footwear - no thick sole, steel-toed work boots. It is almost mind-blowing that every person in that country is not wealthy. They aren't because of the corruption involved with selling the contracts to mine those minerals.

A STUDENT SENT an email once to a fellow teacher from the Democratic Republic of Congo. He asked for a waiver for a required standardized test. The only testing center was in the most northwestern corner of the country and he lived in the most southeastern corner. Travel conditions were unsafe. We verified, and what the student said was all true. After checking this place on Google Earth, we agreed that we wouldn't ask anyone to risk their life for a test score.

THUS, I can conclude that the self-organization quality of a system, while extremely valuable, can turn into harmful.

Hierarchy

SYSTEMS CAN BE DIVIDED into smaller subsystems. For example, in a forest ecosystem, you have living things. You can break this down into the subsystems of plants and animals. If you look at the animals, you can further divide them into mammals, birds, reptiles, amphibians, and insects.

TAKING JUST one of those subsystems, mammals, you could break it down into animals like squirrels, bears, rabbits, and deer. Look at one individual mammal within the taxonomic index. You will find it has a kingdom, genus, and species. You can zoom on concrete details about the animal, plant, bacteria, protozoa indexed. This is a system hierarchy in action. [9]

LIVING systems are not the only ones using hierarchies. You find this type of organization in corporations, the military, financial institutions, government, education, and so many others. Why? Because it works.

ORGANIZATION THROUGH HIERARCHY can serve as a stabilizing force in a system and lead to greater efficiency and productivity. In 2013 Croatia joined the European Union, becoming the 28th member of the organization. The EU then consisted of 28 countries, each having its own governments. (Since then, Brexit happened, so now they are down to 27 members.) These governments consist of a prime minister and/or a president, ministers, and local governments. These subsystems are all working individually, but they depend on the larger systems above them to meet the desired goals of the union.

. . .

LIVING things are perfectly designed by nature to exist through the hierarchy of systems and subsystems. Let's look at a mammal, for example. Cells survive and multiply on their own. That subsystem works together to make and support tissues, which work together to create and support organs. Those organs work together to make and support other organs and systems such as the gastrointestinal system, cardiothoracic system, or neurological system. Those organs, systems, and other subsystems work together to create and support an organism. Then the organism is part of a larger species living together. Those species are part of a larger ecosystem living and working together. These smaller subsystems, even down to the smallest cells, can support themselves. They also work together to help meet the needs of the larger subsystems and overarching system above them in the hierarchy at the same time. The umbrella system acts as the conductor of an orchestra. It ensures that the subsystems work together and that their functions coordinate to make the whole system a strong, stable, successful, resilient, and well-functioning one.

. . .

ALL OF THE subsystems are connected within the system, but each subsystem has its closest connections within. Think about it like the people at a baseball game. The players, coaches, umpires, fans, ushers, concession employees, announcers, grounds crew, parking attendants, security guards, ticket takers, and others are all part of the baseball game system. They all work together to create the experience and atmosphere of the game. Each subsystem is responsible for a specific purpose within the overarching system. Even though they are all connected to each other, the strength of those connections is not equal between all of them. The players, coaches, and fans of team A will be much closer and more connected to each other than they will be to any other subsystems, especially those who are a part of team B. But even in the subsystem of team A, the players will be more connected to each other than their fans, right? The ground crew members will be more strongly connected to each other than they would be to the concession employees. They work more closely and spend more time together.

HIERARCHIES EVOLVE BOTTOM-UP, from part to whole. The foundational guiding purpose of a hierarchy is to help the smaller subsystems function better and have the support they need. This, in turn, serves the system as a whole because if the little parts do their jobs better, the entire system will benefit and perform more efficiently.

IN MANY CASES, the hierarchy levels forget that they need to work together and aim to achieve everyone's goals. That's why some hierarchies are poorly functioning, and the system's goals aren't met.

SOMETIMES SUBSYSTEMS THINK of their purpose as being more important than that of the whole system. Achieving their goals comes at the expense of and detriment to the entire system. This process is called sub-optimization.

CONVERSELY, suppose the top levels of the hierarchy control the lower levels to the extent that they are prevented from carrying out their functions. In that case, the system as a whole will suffer the same sub-optimization.

. . .

A HIGHLY FUNCTIONING system is a lot like a democracy. In the United States, the freedoms and rights of citizens and laws in individual states are protected and encouraged even if they undermine the federal law. Many states have, in the past few years, legalized medical and recreational marijuana usage. Marijuana usage is still federally illegal. You can transport weed over state lines, but the states retain more self-governance than the federal government.

THE CENTRAL GUIDING force that the entire government system must follow is the United States Constitution. Freedoms are afforded to the representatives from the House and Senate to pass laws and represent their constituents in Washington. While the US has a relatively powerful federal government, the real power has always been with the states. The Federal government's power extends only to what is expressed in the constitution (which is a living, breathing document - it changes) or what it has usurped and not been called out on.

EVENT LEVEL VS. **Behavior Level Analysis**

. . .

WHEN WE TALK of a system's behavior, we look at how it performs over time. Has it grown, stayed the same, or declined? Is it well-organized or random? How has it evolved and changed?

IF YOU LOVE READING about history, you know that retrospective data on a given historical event makes the outcome predictable for historical analysts of today. Let's take the Roman Empire as an example. While the central authority was strong and united, the empire was invincible. It operated with an organizational system that could keep its tens of millions of subjects under control. The empire was facing external threats, attacks by the Goths in the north and the Parthians in the south, but they overcame adversities and thrived. It wasn't until the death of Emperor Commodus in 192 AD and the death of the Antoninus Dynasty that the empire started to decline, slowly but surely. [10] Since Commodus had no heirs and hadn't appointed anyone to take his place, chaos and individual greed began to overtake the system's goal as a whole. Namely to keep together and enrich the Roman Empire. One hundred and eighty-four years after the death of Commodus, in 476 AD, the Roman Empire collapsed.

. . .

THE FALL of a great empire is not unique. Before the Romans, the Macedonian Empire of Alexander the Great suffered the same fate. Centuries later the Napoleon's First French Empire ended up sharing the experience of the Romans. The common feature in all these stories is that while subsystems worked toward the whole system's benefit and the system provided the subsystems their needs, these great empires were undefeatable. When this balance changed, the empire-systems collapsed. An interesting exception that empowers the rule is the British recovery from the loss of all their colonies. While the British Empire collapsed, their home base remained independent and not taken over by an external invader. The British colonial empire doesn't exist anymore, yet Britain didn't wither and die. It's still a strong and powerful nation. It thrived differently while also managing the loss of its colonies — and what those colonies provided.

LOOKING at the Roman Empire's timeline, or the empire of Alexander the Great, we can highlight the rise, the peak, and the downfall of each of them. But what would happen if we only looked at Commodus' death or a single successful conquest of Alexander? Could we predict or have a clear picture of the empire's behavior just by one event? Not really, right?

WHEN WE STUDY individual events superficially, in isolation, we won't get answers to questions like "what now?" or "what will happen to the country?" or "how will this event affect the economy?" Like in history, today, we won't get accurate information by putting one event under the microscope. To get the answers we seek, we need to dig deeper and make a behavior over time analysis.

SYSTEMS THINKERS automatically look for historical data and when presented with a problem. They want to know if the system has ever been in the same position before. Then they study the data and look for patterns. Studying long-term behavior is a window into the underlying structure of the system. It can reveal a wealth of information about what is happening in it, and more importantly, why it is happening. Only then can we get to the heart of a problem and uncover a possible improvement.

. . .

A SYSTEM'S structure is formed by its stocks, flows, and feedback loops. The structure is made visible through causal loop diagrams, completed with boxes, arrows, and thought bubbles. The diagrams will show what behavior tendencies a system has. When we encounter a balancing feedback loop, we can conclude that the system is working toward maintaining or establishing a dynamic equilibrium. A reinforcing feedback loop indicates exponential growth or decline.

FOOTBALL GAMES ARE a good example of event-level analysis. Perhaps you have heard of Monday Morning Quarterbacks. They are the people who are eager to offer their opinions and commentary, usually quite critically, on the performance of a player or team in a football game that occurred over the previous weekend. They do not hesitate to judge the performance of others once the game has happened. They usually complain to their friends or call into radio shows offering their opinions without attempting to dig deeper and study the history behind the performance. While this analysis may be entertaining, it is more superficial. It does little to help us predict what will happen in future games.

I MUST ADD in MMQ's defense that a lot of this information is top secret. The NE Patriots won't release videos of their practice drills to the general public. They don't want other teams prepping to their strategies. The other team only gets previous game-play videos to strategize with. Meanwhile, each team takes extensive videos of their practice drills. They break down each play and analyze it to death, so each team member knows their part backward and forward. It hopefully goes off seamlessly and without an injury.

ON THE OTHER HAND, coaches, medical staff, sideline reporters, and seasoned analysts of the game would make every effort to look for long-term behavior and patterns to explain the player or team's performance. They would look at injury reports, study game tapes - both current and past - and conduct interviews. They study statistical data to assess whether the team had been in the same or a similar position before. This will give a more complete picture and explanation of the reasons behind the performance.

THE NONLINEAR WORLD

MUCH TO THE chagrin of our linear-thinking minds, we live in a nonlinear world. Systems often surprise us when they react and perform in nonlinear ways. In the realm of linear thinking, an action will have a consequence – small action, small consequence, big action, big consequence. This isn't always the case in nonlinear systems. If you add a small stimulus or push in a system, you will sometimes get a triple-sized response.

WHEN THE ELECTION season is upon us, the candidates running for office in both parties begin to roll out their advertisements to convince voters to support them. They send flyers through the mail, place signs on billboards and yards throughout their campaign area, and hold rallies. Representatives go door-to-door to speak on their behalf, make phone calls to people within their political party, increase their social media presence, and run commercials on television and radio stations. Some advertising can be good for making potential voters aware of them and their message, and possibly increase the number of votes they receive. But it is also possible that too much advertising will have the opposite effect. It can cause voters to become annoyed and makes them less likely to vote for them in the election.

OR CONSIDER AN AVALANCHE. AVALANCHES "NEED" three parts to happen: snow, a sloped surface, and a trigger. A weak layer within the snowpack, caused by ice, surface, or depth hoar, if meeting a trigger such as a minimal amount of fresh snow or a little motion, can release a cascade of destructive snow down the side of a mountain.

Nonlinearities confuse us because they challenge our expectations regarding what type of response we will get from taking a particular action. Nonlinearities are capable of causing the entire behavior of a system to flip and change course because they change the relative strength of feedback loops.

. . .

WHEN YOU SEE a sudden movement from a time of great growth caused by a powerful reinforcing feedback loop to a time of decline caused by a controlling, balancing feedback loop, nonlinearities are at work.

IN HIS ARTICLE Overview of Systems Thinking, written in 1996, Daniel Aronson gives a good example of how systems thinking can help overcome the problem of nonlinearities. [11] Recall the example where insects were eating farmers' crops. The traditional method, spraying pesticides on the crops to kill the insects, led to undesired consequences. Aronson asks us to imagine a perfect pesticide is used that doesn't have any of the potential environmental concerns that pesticides currently do.

A SIMPLE DIAGRAM would show that as a pesticide is applied, the number of insects goes down. To someone who thinks results are linear, the assumption would be that as more pesticides are applied, more insects will be killed and the crops will be saved. This thesis can prove to be true in the short term.

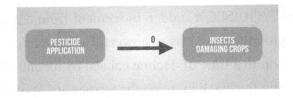

DIAGRAM 8: The relationship between pesticide application and the insects[12]

ON THE DIAGRAM, the arrow indicates the direction of the intervention. "O" means that there is a change happening in an "opposite" direction. When one side goes up, the other side goes down. If we had the letter "s" above the arrow, it would mean that change is happening in the same direction: When one side goes up, the other side will go up too and vice versa. [13]

A SYSTEMS THINKER knows that jumping to conclusions based on an individual event won't answer long-term questions. There are countless nonlinearities in the world. Often, suppose we rush to embrace a quick solution to a problem. In that case, we often do not consider unintended negative consequences that can result from our actions.

OVER TIME, if we continue to apply pesticides to the crops, they will cause more damage than the insects. Why is this? By failing to look at all of the potential consequences of a possible solution, we may inadvertently cause the very result that we were trying to avoid in the long term. As we spray pesticides, we will kill the original insect that was eating the crops. But in doing so, we will also tamper with nature's delicate balance. Once the insects have been killed, other insects in the area will increase in number. This is either due to the first insect no longer being around to act as competition. Or no longer being around to act as a predator keeping the other populations of insects in check from growing too big.

WHEN THE OTHER insects increase in number, they will eat even more of the crops. As a result, our actions caused the problem to get worse in the long run.

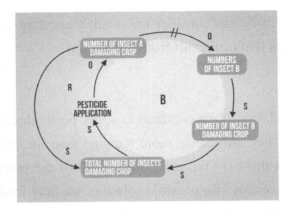

Diagram 9: The balancing (B) and reinforcing (R) feedback loops of the pesticides[14]

Take a look at the diagram. According to the feedback loop and our short-term expectations, the more pesticide we apply, the fewer insects will destroy our crops. (Insect A is the original insect we want to get rid of). But the decrease of insect A inadvertently leads to a boom of insect B. (Notice the "o" - opposite direction.) The increase in the number of insect B will lead to more damage to our crops. The more insects there are, the more damage they create. This change happens in the "s" – same direction. We reached our goal in the short-term and diminished the number of the original insects (insect A). In the long-term, however, the total number of insects damaging our crops increased. Suppose we keep responding to the increased numbers of insects with more pesticides. In that case, we'll only reinforce the loop we are already in.

SYSTEMS THINKERS STUDY potential problems creating a detailed causal loop diagram like Diagram 9. They spend time exploring the problem and all possible solutions from every angle to be sure they aren't surprised by unintended negative consequences. This way, they can design more creative and better solutions.

IN THE CASE OF PESTICIDES, Aronson suggests that systems thinkers would have been more likely to develop a solution like introducing more of the original insect's natural predators into the area. This would have caused their numbers to drop, but not so dramatically that the other insect populations would get out of control. The crops would have been more protected in the long run. [15]

OPEN SYSTEMS HAVE NO BOUNDARIES.

. . .

ALL SYSTEMS ARE CONNECTED. There are no separate individual systems. This is a difficult concept to wrap our heads around. Boundaries are artificially created by people to help them separate and clearly examine one problem at a time. There is no such thing as one correct boundary of a system. The boundaries we decide to draw around systems are based on the questions we are trying to answer and the problems we are trying to solve.

THE BOUNDARIES we draw can lead to problems if we fail to keep in mind that they are of our own making and were artificially created by us. Ideally, we would study a problem and choose whatever boundary best helped to meet the system's needs. But we are creatures of habit. We become comfortable with the boundaries we typically use. To get a more accurate picture, we should create a new boundary for each problem, have an open mind, and judge every situation on its own merits.

THE LIMITS **of a system**

Just because systems don't have boundaries, it doesn't mean they have no limits. There are limits around every system. Our challenge as systems thinkers is to figure out what those limits are and recognize that growth either diminishes or intensifies them. When one factor in a system is no longer limiting, there will be growth. That growth will impact other elements, either making them more plentiful or sparse until one of those factors becomes the new limiting influence on the system.

MOVING our focus from the plentiful factors to the next potentially limiting factor is what understanding and ultimately controlling the growth of a system is all about. As systems grow and develop over time, they interact with each other and impact their own limits. This creates a coevolving dynamic system.

A DEEPER UNDERSTANDING of the limits currently in place in a system and the next potentially limiting factor is not enough to guarantee that the system will continue to grow forever. That isn't possible. Just think about population growth, income growth, or even body mass growth. None of these can go on forever. Instead of focusing on achieving never-ending growth, it's more useful to establish minimum requirements and acceptable limits the system can live in.

UNIVERSITIES ALWAYS WANT to attract more students. They work to create a learning and campus environment that results in happy students. They will spread the word to others about what a great place it is to go to school there, and more students will enroll. While the university would like to see this growth continue indefinitely, there will ultimately be a time limit that prevents them from bringing in more students. The biggest issue with on-campus student enrollment we've had over the past five years is that classes are taught during certain hours and specific schedules. The ability to find space to teach courses in rooms outside specific areas has gotten harder and harder – to the point where school starts in a week, and I have a class with twenty students enrolled and no assigned meeting space. Going online removes that space issue and limits the number of students per cohort or per section for QC issues. You can teach multiple sections or run multiple cohorts in a year. Another limit to growth can be the financial aid and scholarships because there is only a single federal student loan lender now – The US government. All other companies are just processors, and those are limited.

We need to accept that there will always be limits to a system's growth. These limits will either be self-imposed or system-imposed. No system can grow forever. If people do not choose to put their own limits in place, the system will automatically do it for them.

DELAYS

Everything takes time. System changes are no exception. Delays are inevitable. Stocks have delays. Many flows have delays as well. Whenever you ship something, there is a processing time. That is a form of delay. Whenever you send an email, and the recipient reads it a day later, is a perception delay. Some things have even more significant delays. For example, a change in the incentives to encourage childbirth and rearing in a country wanting to increase its population growth won't show its positive or negative effects for years. People have a perception delay – not everybody will know about the new incentives right away or be ready to bear and rear children when the incentives are announced. There will be a natural, biological delay. Optimally, it takes nine months for a child to be born. It will take months or years to measure longitudinal population growth, analyze the data, conclude that the increase (if there is any) is due to the policy changes. Delays are a fact of life in systems.

WHEN WE CHOOSE what delays to examine in a system, we should focus on our current questions and concerns. Suppose we are interested in analyzing fluctuations or swings that are happening over months. In that case, delays that take minutes or years should not be our immediate concern.

DELAYS ARE the driving forces behind how fast systems can respond to change. Delays are responsible for causing declines, overshoots, and fluctuations within a system. [16]

BOUNDED **Rationality as referred to by Nobel Prize-winning economist Herbert Simon.**

. . .

THEODORE ROOSEVELT ONCE SAID, "Do what you can with what you have where you are." This could be a fair summary of what bounded rationality is. It means that people usually make sensible decisions based on the information they have available. The quality of their decisions is only as good as the information they have. It is impossible to have perfect information, especially about distant parts of a system. Farmers don't know how much rain to expect in a given year, if there be drought, or how the economy will shift. Farmers can only be sure of their sowing and reaping methods and their plants' or animals' caretaking.

A FAMOUS QUOTE by Robert H. Schuller illustrates this point well. He said, "Anyone can count the seeds in an apple, but only God can count the number of apples in a seed." An apple orchardist can study data from the yields of his trees over time and carefully analyze all aspects of his orchard system. But try as he might, he will never successfully predict the exact number of apples that will grow from each of the seeds (trees) he plants.

. . .

NOBEL PRIZE-WINNING economist Herbert Simon explained in his theory of bounded rationality that we are not all-knowing beings. He recognized that there are limits on our decision-making abilities, including our intellectual and reasoning abilities. The quality of the information we have and the amount of time we have before the decision must be made are key to success. People make decisions by what Simon refers to as satisficing: doing the best they can with what they have.

WE CAN'T PREDICT what others will do in a given situation. This limits our ability to see every possibility that lies ahead of us and hinders our decision-making abilities. We have to try to make the best decision we can and then move on to the next one.

WE ARE HUMAN, and we make mistakes even in processing and interpreting the information we have access to. We have to do our best to be open-minded and objective as we analyze data.

. . .

OUR DECISIONS ARE ONLY as good as the information we have. We need to expand the amount of information we have access to and review. This means gathering data from the entire system instead of just certain elements. Suppose the information is not accessible in the system. In that case, it needs to undergo some changes to ensure access to the best possible information.

WHEN TO INTERVENE IN A SYSTEM?

In the previous section, I discussed changing the system to gain better information. You may be asking yourself, "how can I change the system? Where should I intervene? How?" I will answer these questions now.

LEVERAGE POINTS

HOW CAN we change a system's structure? How do we access more and better information? Ultimately, how can we make the system produce more of the things we want and less of the things we don't? We

need to start by finding the system's leverage points.
17

LEVERAGE POINTS ARE the parts in a system where making a small change could result in a big difference in behavior. We don't have to change much to have a big impact. The problem is that people often don't push the change in the right direction. We need to consider a cost-benefit analysis if we move a leverage point in a specific direction. If we don't, we may aggravate the problem.

REMEMBER THE EXAMPLE OF PESTICIDES? Using them was not the best leverage point. Interfering in the balance of nature caused more damage to the crops in the long run. Recall my example with the avalanche. A good leverage point is like hitting the spot on a mountain and cause the largest avalanche. Just as the Disney character, Mulan, did with the Chinese Army's last cannon in an attempt to use nature to defeat the Huns. (If you have children around the age of twenty-five - thirty, you must know what I'm talking about.)

· · ·

CHANGING **parameters**

A parameter is a characteristic that helps to define and evaluate a system. When we alter the guidelines by which we judge the success of a system, it can result in significant changes.

EVERY TIME we enter a new election cycle, the national debt becomes a major topic of debate between candidates of both political parties. The national debt is a stock. If the government spends more money or cuts taxes, the national debt increases. If the government cuts spending or raises taxes, the national debt decreases (as long as the increase is greater than the interest payments our country has to make). Our elected officials have to make difficult decisions to adjust the flows into and out of this system.

THESE DECISIONS ARE MADE ALL the more difficult because our government officials like to get reelected. The national debt is always a hot button, politically charged issue. Both parties blame each other and argue over the parameters that impact the debt's size. The voters are invested in this system's monetary flows because they are responsible for paying for the debt. Everyone will tell you that they want the debt to drop, but they do not want to pay more in taxes or have any government programs that are important to them cut to reduce spending. This causes hesitation and anxiety for the government officials because they don't want to upset their constituents so much that they won't reelect them. This approach results in the debt gradually growing no matter who is in office.

PARAMETERS ARE important but only in the short term. Voters feel passionate about them if they are directly impacted by the flows. They will make their voices heard on things like wanting subsidies to help pay for rising healthcare or having to pay more in taxes. But changing the parameters in a system rarely results in positive change to how our national economy behaves. They aren't strong enough to bring stability to the system as a whole. Overall, changing parameters in a system is not a quick or impactful way of intervention.

. . .

BUFFERS

A stock that acts to stabilize a system is known as a buffer. Buffers are an added support in place to help a system to stay steady when things go wrong. A buffer is the money in our savings account to help protect us if we have an unexpected expense or run into financial difficulties. We want to have enough batteries and candles in our home in case our power goes out. Or enough food in our pantry in case we can't make it to the store. All of these stocks act as buffers.

IF WE INCREASE the size of the buffer, we get more stability in our system. There is a fine line, though. If our buffer's size becomes too large, we risk having an unyielding and stagnant system resistant to change. For example, if you hoard together a big food supply, you'll need to consume that over time if you don't want it to expire.

THINKING ON A LARGER SCALE, power plants and water reservoirs work as buffers. Big buffers like those respond slowly. Repairing and expanding them takes time, and they are not cheap to maintain. Since they are slow to react and resistant to change, they do not make good leverage points. [18]

RULES AND INCENTIVES

A system's rules define the area it is tasked to work within, its limits, and how much freedom it has. Rules are powerful. When rules change or are restructured, our behavior responds very quickly and changes right along with them. If the speed limit suddenly changes from 75 Mph to 70 Mph, we'll automatically adapt to the slower driving speed to avoid speeding tickets. This makes rule changes excellent leverage points. Those who can change the rules hold a great deal of power in their hands.

WHEN THINGS GO wrong or right in a system, and you are trying to find out why, take a look at the rules in place and who can make those rules.

6

Examples Of One And Two-Stock Systems

The examples I'm about to discuss are classic systems thinking examples.

A ONE STOCK **System - Population and the industrial economy**

Let's take a look at what happens when a reinforcing loop and a balancing loop are both pulling on the same stock?

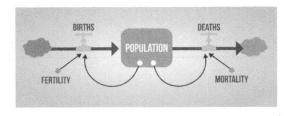

DIAGRAM 10: A stock pulled by a reinforcing (R) and balancing (B) loop[1]

ALL POPULATIONS HAVE A REINFORCING loop that allows them to grow through their birth rate and a balancing loop that indicates mortality. If the birth rate is higher than the death rate, the population increases as the reinforcing loop is in control. If the death rate is higher than the birth rate, the balancing loop is dominant, and the population decreases for that year.

LET'S take a population of thirty giraffes. During a year and a half, the giraffes welcomed nine new babies into their herd, while five giraffes died. Since the birth rate was higher than the death rate, the reinforcing loop was dominant, and resulted in population growth.

DURING THE FOLLOWING year and a half, deforestation occurs. This causes eleven giraffes to die while they have only four newborns. The balancing loop would be in control in this case. The number of giraffes in the herd would decrease.

IF THE BIRTH rate and death rate were the same – seven giraffes were born and seven giraffes died during the same period – the giraffe population would enter a state of dynamic equilibrium.

THE BEHAVIOR in the example of the giraffe population demonstrated the shifting dominance of feed-back loops. The dominant loop has the most influence on the system and its behavior. When two or more feedback loops affect the system simultaneously, they compete with one another, and the dominant loop is the one that determines the behavior. When the reinforcing loop was dominant, the population responded with growth. When the balancing loop is in control, the population declined. When both the reinforcing and balancing loop are of the same strength, the system is in dynamic equilibrium.

WHENEVER YOU ARE PRESENTED with a prediction, you will want to dig deeper to see if there is a reliable forecast based on data. The following questions are helpful to consider as you evaluate a prediction:

•"ARE the driving factors likely to behave in the way they suggest?"

In our example, the driving factors are the birth and death rates. This is a hard question to answer with certainty because it asks you to make a guess about the future. The best a systems thinker can do is carefully study the system's behavior over time. Explore what would happen if the driving factors behaved in various ways - studying all possible scenarios. Making predictions in a dynamic system without proper exploration is not a good idea.

. . .

•"IF THE DRIVING factors did behave that way, would the system react this way?"

In our example, we would ask if the birth and death rates would make the stock (population) respond the way we think it would? This question is a test of the accuracy of the model we use. Regardless of what you believe the driving factors will do, would the system behave as expected?

•"WHAT IS DRIVING THE DRIVING FACTORS?" [2]

In our example, we would examine what is impacting the birth and death rates. This question assesses the boundaries of a system. It examines the driving factors to see if they are acting autonomously or are implanted in the system. There will be multiple forces impacting the driving factors (birth and death rates) from both within and outside the system. While the driving factors are themselves feedback loops, they are also influenced by the feedback loops acting upon them.

Let's bring the giraffes into the zoo with many other kinds of animals to demonstrate how economic factors can influence population. Just like the population, the economy is a reinforcing loop-balancing loop system. It has the same structure and behavior patterns as a population.

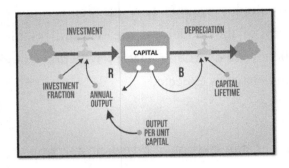

DIAGRAM 11: The behavior of the economy.[3]

A ZOO MAKES money from the people who purchase tickets to visit it. The greater the zoo's stock - the number of animals, attractions, vending machines, cafes, and gift shop items - and the efficiency of their production, the more output (goods and services to guests) it will produce over time. In Picture Diagram 11, this is illustrated by the capital stock box. A zoo operating at a large scale is likely to have a breeding program. That is an inflow. Some inflows may be payments from other zoos for purchases of animals to bread at their zoo.

SUPPOSE the zoo produces a lot of output, like offering more shows and attractions, souvenirs, and food for their visitors to buy. In that case, they will generate more income, which they can then reinvest back into the zoo. By reinvesting that capital, they will be able to purchase, feed, and care for more animals, build and make improvements to their attractions and facilities, hire more employees, and buy more food and souvenirs to sell, etc. This will help them make even more income. This is a reinforcing loop that works just like the birth rate reinforcing loop in our previous example. The more output the zoo can reinvest, the faster it will grow its stock of physical capital. We can see this process on Diagram 11 where there is a dominant reinforcing feedback loop (R) of the output reinvested, ensuring stable growth.

NOT ONLY GROWTH can happen to a business. If they become injured, sick, or even die, the animals that decline in the stock would act as the population example's death rate. Every attraction and facility depreciates and suffers from wear and tear over time or becomes less popular with guests. This may mean they can no longer be used by the zoo. The longer the zoo can take good care of everything and keep using their physical capital, the less capital they will need to lose each year. On Diagram 11, we can see this process through the balancing feedback loop (B) that affects the depreciation.

IF THE ZOO'S reinforcing loop is dominant, it will reinvest money back into the system and assure further growth. If the zoo's balancing loop is in control, the zoo will have to retire and replace more capital instead of increasing its stock. This will result in the growth slowing down or dying off. Suppose neither the reinforcing nor the balancing loop is dominant. In that case, the system will level off and stay in a state of dynamic equilibrium. Whether this system grows, dies off, or remains constant depends on:

•how much output the system invests,

•how efficiently can the capital create a unit of output,

•the lifespan of the capital.

. . .

THERE ARE two ways to make a stock grow: increase its inflow or reduce its outflow. In our zoo example, the stock could grow if more animals, food, souvenirs, attractions, and facilities were purchased (increasing the inflow). Or by taking such good care of the existing capital that it would not have to be retired or replaced for as long as possible. This reduces outflow.

SYSTEMS CAUSE THEIR OWN BEHAVIOR. Systems with the same structure will exhibit the same dynamic behaviors even when you think they couldn't be more different. Both the economy and population can reproduce themselves – money makes money, and giraffes make giraffes. Giraffes age and die. Money loses its value over time due to inflation. The paper the money is made of ages, and becomes unusable. The physical paper money needs to be changed.

IN THE LARGE-SCALE view of economic development, analyzing population and economic growth together is one of the most important research topics investigated. The answer these researchers seek is how to make the reinforcing loop of capital creation work faster than the reinforcing loop of population growth. In other words, if the population grows faster than wealth, people will get poorer. If a country's or the general commonwealth grows faster than the population, people will live better. This, of course, is an incomplete model that assumes that wealth distribution is equal. In reality, wealth distribution is far from being equal. In real life, the rich get richer, and the poor get poorer. How and why? I will talk about it in the following chapters.

A RENEWABLE STOCK **Constrained by a Nonrenewable Stock** [4]

IN OUR PREVIOUS EXAMPLES, we talked about the population and the economy. These were both examples of one-stock systems. Now I will present a system that has two stocks, a renewable and a nonrenewable.

EVERYTHING tangible in this world exchanges things with the environment surrounding it. A school needs students, teachers, water, and electricity to function. An animal needs food, water, shelter, and habitat to survive. Because of biological, physical, and chemical needs, growing systems influenced by a reinforcing loop will ultimately encounter a limitation. This will take the form of a balancing loop. Even when a balancing loop isn't dominant, we know its existence because it's impossible for any physical system to keep growing forever. Systems theory calls this phenomenon the "Limits-to-growth" archetype.

RESOURCES PROVIDE inflow to the stock, and they are either renewable or nonrenewable. Renewable resources are oxygen, water, wind, and solar energy. These can be used over and over. Nature replicates them before they are completely consumed. Nonrenewable resources are coal, oil, and natural gases that take a long time to be replaced by nature. They can't be replaced as fast as they are being used. It's important to make the same distinction with pollutants, which can also be renewable or nonrenewable. A pollutant is renewable if the environment has a fixed ability to remove it. A pollutant is nonrenewable if the environment cannot absorb the pollutant or make it less harmful. [5]

. . .

LET'S see the behavior of an oil company on Diagram 12.

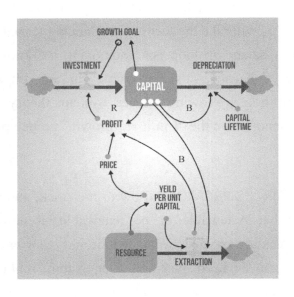

DIAGRAM 12: A Renewable Stock Constrained by a Nonrenewable Stock[6]

THE BALANCING LOOP (B1) drives depreciation and represents the company's machinery, such as the extracting and refining equipment. Suppose we estimate an average lifetime of about twenty-five years for these machines. In that case, this means the oil company will lose 1/25 of its capital stock each year.

In other words, four percent of this company's commission will be gone on the very first day of operation.

THIS SYSTEM GROWS when a reinforcing loop (R) is dominant. By reinvesting its profit (income – cost), the oil company will extract more oil. This will lead to a more significant profit that can, again, be reinvested to keep the growth going faster.

OIL IS A NONRENEWABLE RESOURCE, so the stock fostering the extraction doesn't have an input. As you can see in diagram 12, the oil box only has an output. If an oil company removes all the oil, the oilfield becomes depleted. With each barrel of oil they mine, the job of the oil company becomes more difficult. When they drill for each additional barrel, they will have to dig deeper because the stock has decreased. There is less natural pressure to force more oil closer to the surface. The company has to spend more money to effectively mine the leftover oil.

. . .

THIS ACTS as another balancing loop on the system that limits the growth of its capital (B2). When the oil company has a lot of money, it can extract a lot of oil. The more oil it extracts, the more money it will make. But conversely, the more oil it mines, the less oil will remain - and the more expensive it will get to mine. The company will get less yield from each unit of capital they spend. This means that they will make less profit (for this example, we assume that the price they can charge for a barrel of oil remains constant). Thus they will have less money to reinvest, which means their capital will grow slower.

WHEN THE OIL company first starts to drill, there is enough supply. If the difficulty and cost of extraction didn't increase, the extractable oil would last for 100 years. But the actual depletion time depends on many factors like consumption over time, the speed and amount of extraction per year, the number of drills, etc. The extraction will reach its optimal limit quicker than expected due to the increasing extraction costs, causing the extraction to slow down, having less yield per unit of capital. The company will reach a point where the costs will be so significant that the income they earn from extracting another barrel isn't enough to keep the investment ahead of depreciation. The capital stock decreases, and the drilling shuts down, abandoning the oil left in the ground because the extraction cost wouldn't be worth the gains. The same happens with any system whose growth depends on nonrenewable resources. The faster the system grows in such cases, the faster it will fall. The ultimate decision a company has to make in the case of a nonrenewable resource is to get rich quickly or stay in business longer.

THIS EXAMPLE WAS a simplification of the real world, of course. We assumed that oil prices stay constant, no new oil field is discovered, and no natural event affects the extraction process. We also didn't consider the negative natural consequences a fast extraction can cause. Let's imagine what would happen if oil prices increased. In this case, the company would have more profit to invest in faster extraction. The critical point when the oil extraction was not worth the cost would come later. Conversely, if oil prices dropped, the company would be out of business quicker.

. . .

THERE ARE two ways to increase stocks: by increasing the inflow or by reducing the outflow. In the case of our oil company, reducing the outflow might be caused by technological advances, making it cheaper and easier to extract the remaining oil from the field. The company's operating costs would drop.

AS LONG AS systems depend on nonrenewable resources to grow their stock, depletion dynamics will be in play. An oil company knows that the oil supply in a field will become depleted and too costly to extract, causing them to abandon it. They are always on the lookout for the next place they can drill. The larger the stock of oil they have to begin with, the longer the reinforcing loop will dominate the balancing loop. The higher the capital stock and the cost of extraction, the earlier, faster, and further the fall will be after the system hits its production peak. As they say, the bigger they are, the harder they fall.

BIG OIL COMPANIES know the risks of quick depletion and increased costs, so they start to scout a new oil extraction location before the old one runs out. Think of Halliburton, a vast oil company in

Texas. Oil and gas are one of their biggest industries. Halliburton doesn't drill exclusively in Texas. It also drills in the Middle East. When Halliburton wanted to go into Iraq after its second war with the US to help "rebuild" it was granted many government contracts to do that. (But then Dick Cheney, the Vice President at the time, was also the former CEO of Halliburton.) The point being, big firms look for new opportunities before the nonrenewable resource runs out. [7]

THERE ARE systems where a renewable stock is constrained, and extraction can be limited. A good example is the lumber industry. Trees take time to grow. A renewable source can support extraction indefinitely, especially since a wood exporting company is likely getting lumber from multiple sources. But only with an extraction rate that matches the regeneration rate. Suppose the lumber company doesn't respect the delicate balance of flow and regeneration and overexploits the stock. In that case, the renewable source might become nonrenewable (extinct, in other words).

7

Systems Archetypes

S ystem archetypes are commonly repeating variations of reinforcing and balancing feedback. Each archetype has a typical pattern of behavior over time, structure, and effective interventions.

THESE ARCHETYPES HELP us to understand and diagram the behavior of a system. The more you practice system analysis, the easier you will notice and apply it when hearing an archetypical systems story. [1] Some systems can cause troublesome behavior through their structure. This can take many forms. Some of the behaviors archetypes create include addiction, low performance, and escalation.

. . .

IT ISN'T enough to just recognize the troublemaking structures and understand the problems they cause. They need to be changed.

People often make the mistake of trying to blame other people for the destruction these archetypes cause. In reality, the fault lies within the structure of the system. So what can be done?

WE CAN ESCAPE these -so-called- system traps by being aware of their existence and use that knowledge to avoid getting caught in them. Or if we are in them, change them. We can change the structure by revisiting our goals and developing new ones. We can work with feedback loops to strengthen, weaken, or alter current behavior. We can even add new feedback mechanisms to the system.

THE ARCHETYPES rapidly build system-level awareness and provide a simple and engaging way to communicate about systems. They are easy to understand. The classic archetype stories are an easy means to transfer learning about system issues from one situation to another.

IF YOU MASTER the systems archetypes, you'll be familiar with the storylines and regular behavior patterns. You'll detect them in real-world events and map their structure with ease. Also, by going deeper, you'll be able to improve and enrich the structure of the specific system you'll be analyzing.

THE NINE MOST common systems archetypes are the following:

•Shifting the Burden

•Fixes that Backfire

•Growth and Underinvestment

•Tragedy of the Commons

•Limits to Success

•Accidental Adversaries

•Escalation

•Drifting Goals

•Success to the Successful

I WILL REVIEW four of the nine archetypes mentioned above: the tragedy of the commons, the success to the successful, escalation, and shifting the burden. You can read about the other archetypes in my book, Learn to Think in Systems.

THE TRAGEDY **of the Commons**

THE TRAGEDY of the commons is a trap that appears when there is escalation in a shared, erodible environment.

IN THE UNITED STATES, there is no limit on who can own a car or how many vehicles a person is allowed to own. In fact, in 2016, there were 268.8 million vehicles registered in the United States, with about 95% of households owning at least one car.

. . .

THIS WAS NOT ALWAYS the case. Until the late 1940s, at least 40% of households didn't own a car. They lived mostly in cities and depended on public transportation to get from place to place. Since the 1960s, the number of vehicles owned in the United States has continued to grow.

WHY IS THIS? As people began to move into suburbs, it spread that one could purchase a house for less money and buy a car to commute to work. The highway system continued to grow and improve. Hence, people found it more convenient to drive themselves around. Not to mentions that suburbs didn't have well-operating public transportation.

CAR OWNERS HAVE the commonly shared environment of our roads and highways. They share the need for oil and gas, both nonrenewable resources. Car owners have the freedom to drive themselves anywhere, anytime they want, not being tied to a public transportation schedule. For many, owning a car is even a status symbol.

. . .

THE DOWNSIDE to the increased growth in car ownership is the finite amount of oil and products made available to us on Earth. The oil is consumed fast as there are so many cars on the road. Another problem is that more cars mean more pollution. This can be a contributing factor to climate change and health problems.

ADDITIONALLY, as more cars travel on our roadways, there is increased wear and tear on them. This can render some roads and bridges unsafe to travel on and can result in costly repairs. All taxpayers share the financial burden. Not to mention the insurance costs of drivers who don't carry it despite it being a legal requirement. The increase in cars also means an increase in accidents, which over-whelm emergency rooms. We can see the ripple effect here.

IN THIS EXAMPLE, car ownership has increased in number consistently since the 1960s. Initially, it was encouraged to help financially support the auto industry and touted as a symbol of status. It was a sensible decision for the city banker to own a car because it provided him the freedom to travel as he wished. The only problem was that every other car buyer came to the same conclusion, and soon the highways and roads were invaded with hour-long traffic jams. Some families ended up owning as many as one car per family member. This meant four or five cars per family.

ONE CAR usually has five seats and could efficiently serve a family of five. But due to increased desire for comfort, a high percentage of cars driven on the streets has only one passenger. When a couple works in different areas, and both live far from their work-place, having two vehicles is reasonable.

THE INFRASTRUCTURE of roadways and the highway system continued to grow and improve to serve the growing demand. Car owners understood that if improvements and repairs to roads were neces-sary, everyone would share the cost, so that wasn't a big deterrent to purchasing a car.

HOW TO FIX the tragedy of the commons?

Educate and warn people about the consequences of uncontrolled use of the commons. Make your statements appeal to their morality. Make people aware of the collective costs of their individual actions. Use persuasive language or illustrations to influence peoples' sense of austerity. If sensibility is not motivating enough, use threatening future predictions, mention the possibility of social disapproval. Focus on the greater common good.

PRIVATIZATION CAN BE helpful to save the commons. This way people will need to own their actions and fix whatever they personally damaged. If someone can't control themselves by overexploiting their private resources, they will cause damage mostly to themselves.

REGULATION IS a powerful tool to save the commons. We saw earlier how powerful leverage a change in the rules can be. Bans or restrictions on some behaviors, quotas, taxes, or incentives can all work. Deterring regulations by charging fines or requiring licensing can also be an effective way to stop people from overexploiting the commons. [2]

. . .

SUCCESS **to the successful**

THOSE WHO ARE FINANCIALLY WELL OFF OFTEN use their wealth and privilege to get special treatment and access to goods. This in turn, helps them generate more of the money, privilege, and closed-group information. Competitive exclusion is a system trap.

THINK about what happens when someone wins a competition? They get a reward. This reward — monetary, equipment, access granting, networking, promotions, sponsors — gives the winner the ability to compete even better next time. This forms a reinforcing feedback loop, which increases the likelihood that the winners will keep winning. Consequently, the losers will lose again.

HOW DOES MONOPOLY, the board game, evolve? Each player begins the game on the same level of the playing field. But as soon as a player starts to accumulate properties, the game dynamic changes. When a player controls a property, they can begin to build houses and hotels and charge the other players rent when they land on their properties.

That player can use the other players' money to buy more properties and put more hotels on the game board. This makes it next to impossible for the others to catch up, and dramatically increases the likelihood that the hotel-owning player will win the game.

Monopoly is a strategy game of how you come to own the best-located properties and then make the most money to bankrupt the other players... The player who buys hotels first can only retain exclusive power if they play smart enough to purchase other hotels in strategic locations. The first buyer can control the game only if he keeps growing to other players disadvantaged. (A hotel on Mediterranean Ave is a waste of money if you ask me.)

CONSIDER college football teams in the United States. There is a playoff system that determines the national champion each year. The final four teams play against each other in the playoff. For the past few years, it seems that the same two-three teams monopolized playing in the playoff. As college football teams begin winning games, they are rewarded with more access to television time. This allows them to increase their fan bases, bring more revenue into their programs, and attract more recruits to their teams. As the teams are more visible, they can generate more money through ticket sales and booster donations. This enables them to hire the best coaches and build the best facilities at their schools.

THESE EVENTS ENTICE the best players to join their football programs, which increases the likelihood that they will continue to win and be successful. The reinforcing feedback loop has now become created and entrenched in their systems.

THERE ARE exceptions to this rule, too. Clemson Tigers of South Carolina's Clemson University, which did not even win a conference championship under its previous coach Tommy Bowden, went to winning a national championship under Dabo Swinney in 2017.

. . .

SWINNEY HAD BEEN a coordinator at Clemson before took on the head coach position mid-season in 2008. His greatest asset as a coach is that he is a fantastic recruiter. [3] Alabama has been in the championships since Nick Saban took over in 2007. The success to the successful archetype applies to their case 100 percent. Still, a lot depends on the coach and his coaching and what conference the school plays in. SEC, ACC, Big Ten, Big 12, PAC 12, these all have way more clout. And because the teams aren't playing division II ball in a region where no one cares about college ball. Traditionally these regions are home to the oldest and most prestigious colleges. History brings a lot of rivalry and tradition - and football is one of those rivalries and traditions... Just like sculling at the Ivies and Pacific NW.

WE ALSO SEE the success to the successful archetype at play in nature. The competitive exclusion principle tells us that it is impossible to have two different species living in exactly the same ecological niche, competing for exactly the same food and resources. When two species are different, one species will either be able to reproduce faster or be more effective at using resources than the other species. This will give that species an advantage over the other as it will begin to increase its population and continue to be dominant over the other species. The dominant species does not need to fight the other species. Using up all of the available resources means there are none left for the weaker competitor. This will force that species to either move away, adapt by using different resources, or become extinct.

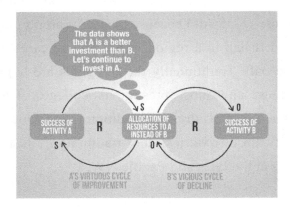

Diagram 13: Success to the successful.[4]

DIAGRAM 13 HAS two reinforcing loops linked by the "allocation of resources" stock. The reinforcing loop on the left (R1) presents the success to the successful scenario. The more resources A allocates, the more he will have to invest, further enriching his stock. The other reinforcing feedback is a vicious cycle of diminishing success for B, the less wealthy.

THE "POOR GET POORER" just the way diagram 13 illustrates. Kids coming from families with fewer resources usually have access to worse education than their wealthy peers. Thus they end up having lower-skilled jobs and lower income levels. Their poverty is reinforced at each stage of life. People who do not have a lot of money are either unable to qualify for loans, or must pay a disproportionately high interest rate compared to the wealthy. This keeps the less wealthy from making investments and improve their futures in the same way the wealthy can. People with low incomes are often unable to own their own homes. [5] They pay rent to those who can afford to own property. Tenants supply landlords, whether with a stable income source or with enough funds to buy a new property for more people to rent. Real-life Monopoly, folks.

THOSE WHO EARN the least tend to pay a more significant percentage of their income to taxes and healthcare. Wealthy individuals have access to attorneys who can help them find loopholes in the tax code and avoid paying a comparable amount of their income in taxes. This being said, I find it essential to mention that the wealthiest one percent of Americans pay the vast majority of American taxes. They pay a smaller percentage, but that percentage still quantifies to a lot of money. The percentage less wealthy people pay will be a larger percentage of their income, but it's a lot less money, practically speaking. The problem doesn't reside only in the taxing system, but in the minimal income some people have. I would gladly pay more taxes if I made double than I do.

OFTEN, people can receive discounts when they purchase items in bulk. Research has found that the "bulk-rule" is generally inaccurate in the case of perishable goods. The average family of four isn't going to use large bulk sizes of items before they spoil. Who is using ten pounds of ranch dressing before it spoils? The only person I can imagine is pouring it in a glass and drinking it. Many bulk purchases go to waste, and thus the person would just be wasting his money while trying to save. [6]

. . .

THIS DOESN'T MEAN purchases at bulk stores don't save money on non-perishable items. Purchases on diapers, meats, and vitamins are all much cheaper, but they are usually slightly larger package sizing. Because the less wealthy are still unable to afford these large purchases, they often have to pay higher per piece prices. Other possible scenarios may have a harder toll on the less wealthy, reinforcing the vicious loop in which they are stuck. They are exposed to more pollution and higher stress levels because they are more likely to rely on public transportation, they breathe in the exhaust of a bus. And who helps with the "poor's" physical and mental diseases? Low-paying jobs don't provide healthcare, yet they take a toll on a person's body and mind.

THE "SUCCESS TO THE SUCCESSFUL" archetype presents only a fraction of reality. Like every other model, it is simplified. It doesn't take into consideration the position of the middle-class, for instance. It's a simplification of reality to illustrate with a visual but extreme example of how the archetype works.

WHAT'S the solution for this scenario?

Sometimes even the appearance of success is enough to get the resources for actual success. Let me illustrate this with a joke.

"A young man wants to marry Bill Gates' daughter. He goes to Bill Gates and asks for his daughter's hand in marriage. The billionaire suspiciously asks the young man:

-Who are you? I will only marry my daughter to the CEO of The Bank of America.

-No problem, says the young man and leaves.

He goes to the Bank of America, applying for the CEO position. When he gets interviewed, the interviewers ask who he is:

-I'm the future son-in-law of Bill Gates, he replies..."

THIS JOKE SHOWS how potential can be confused with or sold as achievement and how the appearance of success is critical to secure future success. When we decide to support one party that can involuntarily cause the decline of other parties, it takes clarity about what actually drives one entity's success or the other's to avoid an unwanted outcome.

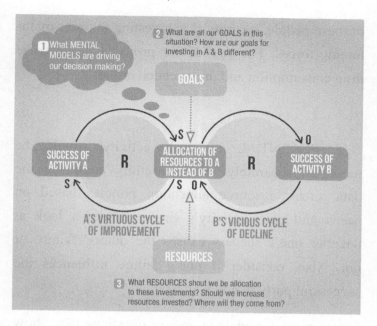

Diagram 14: Possible solutions to fix the success to the successful archetype.[7]

TO CREATE A MORE equal resource allocation, we need to develop awareness on how our present investment decisions influence future investment decisions. Take a look at Diagram 14. The middle stock contains all resources available to invest in activities A and B. Let's say, the problem we are trying to solve is the drug addiction of a disadvantaged group in a poor neighborhood. Activity A is investing in the education of these people. Activity B is investing in order-maintaining forces. The goal of this project is to decrease drug consumption and drug-related crimes.

THE POTENTIAL of each activity should be measured separately. After carefully analyzing the data, create resource allocation policies based on needs and each activity's success. Take a look at whether one's success causes the others' failure or not. Also, consider if one's failure influences the successful party in any way?

Create mental models to answer questions like, "how might we have created a defensive routine? Did we assume one activity is inherently better than the other? where were we biased?" [8]

Answer these questions, use the data, compare everything with the outcome you're seeking. Make changes per your discoveries and get closer to the desired results.

ESCALATION

Have you ever witnessed two siblings fighting with one another? Each new poke, push, or insult is getting worse than the last. In that case, you have seen escalation firsthand.

ESCALATION IS GUIDED by a reinforcing loop in which the actors involved are in competition. The driving factor behind their behavior and decision-making is trying to outdo one another. If the competition brings improvement into the world, we can consider escalation a good thing.

ESCALATION, however, can also be extremely dangerous. When countries around the world race to build up their nuclear weapons faster than others, there can be dire and threatening consequences. The Cold War is an excellent example of negative escalation. Another example is when two people are drag racing. They continue to push harder and harder, trying to beat their competition, prompting them to make more and more careless choices until someone gets hurt.

· · ·

ONE PERVASIVE DISPLAY of escalation in our country and around the world today involves the use of cyberbullying. The internet and social media can be great tools to help make us all interconnected. We can share and access information like never before. But some people feel emboldened by the anonymity that these virtual platforms afford and think they can make any cruel and negative comment about others without consequence. It is rare to read about a recipe or a product review without seeing negative comments designed to offer destructive criticism. They are hurtful and personal. It isn't long before more people begin to argue back and forth, hurling more and more hateful insults at one another. Comments become a means to hurting the other person. The responses from others reading the comments are egging the initial debaters on, encouraging the negative words to continue.

In some cases cyberbullying has such horrifying and dangerous unintended consequences as (teenage) suicide. Some people feel so attacked by their peers and strangers on the internet that they decide to take their own life. They may think they will never be able to escape from the damage that has been done to their reputation. A child, whose brain isn't cognitively formed, can't understand the permanence of suicide. Neither has the experience that life gets better eventually.

NOT ALL SYSTEMS that exhibit escalation are so dire and dangerous. As I said before, escalation can end up being beneficial to our society and the world. The process can lead a group to find groundbreaking scientific discoveries, create helpful inventions in technology, develop new medicines, or find cures for diseases.

THERE IS a reason that escalation is a system archetype. Even in the best situations, escalation can still cause troublesome behavior. No matter the goal or purpose, escalation can grow swiftly, often faster than anyone anticipates. It can result in the competing parties breaking down entirely if nothing is done to break the loop.

HOW TO GET out of an escalating situation?

The best is to avoid engaging in it in the first place. But if you find yourself, or a system, already in an escalating situation, you can try the following things:

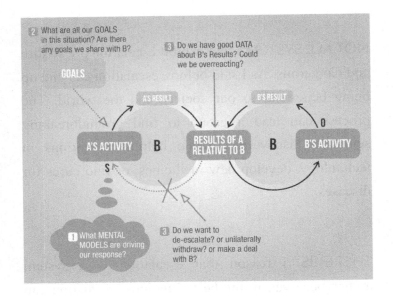

Diagram 15: Possible solutions to escalation.[9]

BECOME aware of the dynamics of the system, its activity level, and the costs.

- Put your thoughts about the escalation under a microscope. What do you think about the escalation?

Is it a zero-sum game? Would the parties be willing to come to an agreement?

- What do you predict will happen if you tried to break the loop and escape this system trap by unilaterally withdrawing from the competition?

- How could each involved party achieve their goals? What are your goals? Do you seek any benefit in this game? Or all that matters to you is outdoing your competitor? If so, can you refocus your objectives?

- Are you sure you have an accurate assessment of your competition? Can you get more accurate information?

- Try to negotiate different system rules using balancing loops to control the reinforcing loop the escalation operates in.

SHIFTING THE BURDEN – **Addiction**

IT'S hard to turn a blind eye to the classic addictions in our society: drugs, alcohol, nicotine, food, shopping, gambling, etc. But there are other kinds of addictions, many that you never thought of as addictions before, present in systems.

ADDICTION IS a reliance or dependence on something. This can be a country receiving government subsidies for financial loans and support. Many areas of our economy receive government subsidies like the energy, agricultural, and transportation sectors, just to name a few. Farmers can have non-negotiable business standards in the form of reliance on pesticides and fertilizers in hopes of more generous yields.

ADDICTIONS CAN INVOLVE BEING dependent on painkillers. Or begin addicted to social validation to feel confident and worthy. No matter the form an addiction takes, the structure of the system looks the same. It has a stock with inflows and outflows. The stock can be something tangible, like crops, or intangible, like self-esteem. The stock's decision-maker adjusts the balancing feedback loop by changing either the inflow or the outflow. [10]

. . .

WHEN INTERVENING IN SUCH CASES, either by granting a subsidy or providing non-material goods, the short-term results can be promising. We may even think that we solved a problem. In reality, by shifting the burden to the intervention, we won't achieve lasting positive results. The subsidy won't last forever. Our bodies will build up a tolerance to painkillers. The same old problems will resurface.

THIS IS because we put a Band-Aid on the problem. We opted for a quick fix without digging deeper to really uncover its root cause and put in the hard work to solve the issue long-term.

DO we have such clarity when a stubborn problem returns? Usually not. We take an extra pain killer. We pour even more money into the farm. The method worked the first time, it will work again. What we're achieving is an increased addiction and dependence on the intervention that weakens the system further.

IN OTHER WORDS, the problem recurs despite our repeated efforts to fix it. Over time, the problem will require more of the "fix" to stay under control. The real cause of the problem is either hard to identify or seems impossible to address.

IT IS best to not fall into the trap of addiction in the first place. But if addiction has taken over, there will be a period of painful withdrawal, whether physical or emotional, to finally break free from the cycle. It will be hard to go to the doctor and discover the real cause of our pain. It will be challenging to tweak our farm to be self-sustaining. But it needs to be done. There is a limit to how many painkillers we can take a day without overdosing. There is a limit to the money one can pour into an underperforming farm.

HOW CAN we avoid the trap?

WHEN IT BECOMES clear that a system requires some outside intervention, step in to help temporarily. Ensure that the intervention is not going to cause dependence in the system. But rather, it will act as a helpful force with ideas on how the system can function on its own and solve its own problems in the future. As soon as the system is strong enough, the intervention should be removed.

IT IS similar to a military strategy when they go into a country needing protection and assistance. The military trains the troops of the country in need, and maintains the peace long enough to stabilize the situation. Then they slowly give the steering wheel back to the country to solve their own problems. "Give a man a fish and you feed him for a day. Teach a man to fish and you feed him for a lifetime."

QUICK FIXES WON'T LAST. The system will have the same problems as before and remain dependent on the intervention. But if you help the system improve to solve its problems, the system will be able to carry on long after the intervention has been removed.

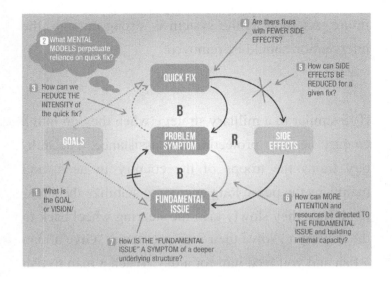

DIAGRAM 16: Possible solutions to the shifting the burden archetype[11]

WHAT IS the goal of the system? Try to clarify it. Allocate the tendency to focus on seemingly urgent symptoms and address the behavior that fosters dependence on the quick fix.

CONSIDERING THE GOALS, weaken or break the connection between the symptom and the quick fix.

Do this by providing as little of a fix as possible. If the symptoms need to be addressed, try to find a substitute fix with fewer side effects or longer-lasting benefits.

IF THE IMPLEMENTATION of short-term solutions is unavoidable, try limiting the consequences as much as you can.

TRY to balance the short-term and long-term solutions. Most often, this means empowering the link between the real problem and the symptom.

ASK YOURSELF IF THE "FUNDAMENTAL ISSUE" is just another symptom? If you confirm this suspicion, dig deeper to identify the addiction's real cause and new ways to address it.[12]

8

Systems Thinking in Social Matters

When we find a gap between where we currently are and where we want to be, we get motivated to change. In a system, in a similar situation, we collectively create a shared vision, mission, and set of core values. That's how we bring meaningful and lasting changes.

WE NEED to make sure everyone is on the same page in evaluating where the system currently is and why it is there. That's when people truly start feeling invested and engaged in wanting to be a part of the solution. They begin to go beyond taking responsibility just for their individual task within the system. They recognize that they also play a role in how the entire system performs. They have more of a stake in the game and will take more ownership over the results.

WHEN TRYING TO SOLVE A PROBLEM, we may end up causing more of the behavior we hope to avoid. As David Peter Stroh, the author of the book Systems Thinking for Social Change[1] says, "organizations and social systems have a life of their own." We might wish to push the system in a positive direction, and the system would still operate the same way as if no intervention had happened. Why? Most probably because it didn't get the right push.

SUPPOSE we don't do our homework and dig deeper into the system to get to the real root of the problem and settle for a quick fix. In that case, we are wasting our time and energy because we won't solve anything.

GOOD INTENTIONS

. . .

BUSINESS CONSULTANT JAMES C. Collins once said, "Bad decisions made with good intentions are still bad decisions." Good intentions are simply not enough. We all mean well, but sometimes in a rush to find a solution, we actually make things worse. It is important to recognize quickly when a solution isn't working. We need to shift gears, learn more about the problem, and try another way of intervention.

HERE ARE JUST a few examples of solutions gone wrong despite everyone's best intentions:

•Countries with the most restrictive abortion laws have the highest rates of abortion. A 2018 study conducted by the Guttmacher Institute found that the abortion rates worldwide have fallen during the last twenty-five years even though more countries have legalized abortion and made the procedure more accessible. Making abortion illegal is intended to decrease the number of women getting abortions, but it seems to have the opposite effect. [2]

•STATES where the death penalty is legal have consistently higher murder rates than states where the death penalty is illegal. The Death Penalty Information Center has gathered statistics on murder rates in all 50 states from 1990-2016 using U.S. Census data and published reports on crime from the F.B.I. During that period, the murder rates were lower in states that did not have the death penalty than states that did. Instituting the death penalty as a possible punishment was intended to deter people from committing heinous crimes like murder. But according to statistics, this is another solution gone wrong. [3]

THERE ARE many more examples of failed solutions that were created with the best of intentions. Increased availability of job training programs didn't result in lower unemployment. The war on drugs contributed to problems it never intended, even as addiction and drug abuse continued to be a significant problem in modern society. There is no shortage of well-intentioned solutions that have failed to bring the results people expected or were promised.

WHEN A JUDGE DECIDES to incarcerate a parent who commits a crime, they do it with good intentions, such as keeping a criminal off the streets and because it's required by the law. (I wish to stress here that I'm talking about minor law infringements. I would never suggest a serial killer, or child abuser be spared just because they have a child.) While the parent is incarcerated, the child will suffer greatly by not having a complete, healthy family and might end up in foster care. Growing up under such circumstances, being in multiple homes feeling unwanted, socioeconomically at risk, and lacking solid values and identity provided by a family unit, may lead this child to a criminal path later in life.

THE JUDGE SHIFTED the burden but created a ripple effect. It is essential to recognize one's contribution to an unwanted consequence. When one recognizes and accepts their responsibility in creating a problem, only then can better solutions be found.

GOOD INTENTIONS ARE NOT ENOUGH. When dealing with complex, chronic social issues, applying conventional linear thinking and quick fixes will not generate the desired lasting solutions. People need to be unified around a shared vision, mission, purpose, and set of goals. They have to do the work of taking a hard, honest, and objective look at where the system currently is. That's how they find better solutions.

THIS UNIFICATION, however, is more complicated than it sounds. It's not like we all agree when we identify a social issue, sit down and sing Kumbaya, My Lord and solve our nation's deepest social crises. It's going to take a lot of work to bring the majority of people to the table to even have a conversation about the problem. This also takes a lot of time. And there will always be outliers who won't join in the conversation. We can't let be stopped by that.

THE INDIVIDUAL RESPONSIBILITY in finding a common solution that takes everybody's needs into consideration is invaluable. It is more than a goal; it's a cause, a purpose. People who are focused and committed put achieving this cause ahead of their own personal interests. They feel empowered to make meaningful and lasting changes. They align their efforts to keep their eyes on the cause, knowing what needs to be done.

. . .

WHEN YOU FIX a system by restructuring it, there can be a period when things worsen before they get better. If you can set up short-term goals aligned with the overarching long-term ones, you might be able to build in some small successes along the way. This helps everyone through the growing hardships and maintains hope that things are moving in the right direction. You can keep up people's motivation to continue working toward achieving the long-term goal. [4]

IN THE FOLLOWING PAGES, we will learn about systems thinking in action. First, however, I would like to do a quick recap on what systems thinking is and how it differs from conventional thinking.

CONVENTIONAL THINKING HAS BEEN our hardwired way of addressing problems. It couldn't be more different from the systems thinking approach. Traditional thinking is looking at things through the lens of cause and effect. It views things as a step-by-step, sequential process with a definite beginning and end. Conventional thinkers believe that it is easy to find the cause of a problem because it's obvious.

They tend to blame people and situations outside of their organization or system when things go wrong. Since they believe others and outside forces need to change, they rarely introspect to find the role they may have played in causing or contributing to the problem.

CONVENTIONAL THINKERS BELIEVE that improving the parts is the way to improve the whole system. A plan leading to short-term success will automatically translate to long-term success in conventional thinkers' understanding. They often work on many strategies independently at the same time, which addresses the symptoms instead of the root of the problem.

IN CONTRAST, systems thinking is a paradigm shift that focuses on asking better questions before jumping to conclusions. Systems thinkers want to get a more complete and accurate picture of the problem before coming up with a solution. They don't believe that the cause of a problem is obvious or quick, and easy to find. People, often unintentionally, create or contribute to their own problems. The power and responsibility to change these problems lie within them instead in outside factors.

SYSTEMS THINKERS KNOW that finding quick fixes to a problem often will either be ineffective or make the problem worse by causing unintended negative consequences. They look to improve the entire system by focusing on and strengthening the relationships between the parts. They believe that focusing on too many strategies at once will scatter focus and won't lead to a lasting change. They would focus all of their attention on implementing a few leverage points that they believe will impact the whole system. They keep working on the chosen change for some time to see if they are effective.

COLLECTIVE IMPACT INTRODUCED **by John Kania and Mark Kramer in the Stanford Social Innovation Review.**

SOCIAL ISSUES ARE chronic and complex. They have been resistant to many solutions offered despite the efforts and best intentions of people for many years. Often in frustration, the strategy tends to be one of "if we throw enough at them, something is bound to stick." Quick, scattered fixes have unintended negative consequences and don't support long-term goals.

COLLECTIVE IMPACT RECOGNIZES that we can achieve more working together than we could ever hope to alone. As described by John Kania and Mark Kramer, this process occurred when a group of community leaders realized that their individual efforts to improve the local public education system didn't have as big of an impact as changing the entire system would. This discovery pushed the leaders to abandon their organizations' individual goals in favor of working collectively on one unifying goal - improving student achievement.

COLLECTIVE IMPACT LEADS TO:

- mutually reinforcing activities,

- a common agenda,

- shared measurement,

- continuous communication. [5]

MUTUALLY REINFORCING activities mean that not everyone has to be doing exactly the same thing. Each person has their own strengths that they bring to the table. But everything has to be coordinated and aligned toward achieving the unified purpose. This process builds trust because participants assure each other of their good intentions, pledging to do the best they can with what they know at the moment.

A COMMON AGENDA INCLUDES:

- a shared vision of change,

- a shared understanding of the problem and its root cause,

- how anyone within the organization may have unintentionally contributed to it,

-and a unified plan of action to solve the problem.

IT IS important to include a realistic view of where the system currently is and why it has gotten there. Some kind of payoff has to be built in the system that kept people perpetuating the problems. Being aware of this inbuilt payoff mechanism is the first step to overcome the old patterns of behavior.

THE COMMON AGENDA offers a distinction between the desired goal and the current payoff system. It becomes obvious to the people involved that change comes with a price and possible sacrifices. They also get a realistic outlook on what can be expected in the future. This way, everyone gets on the same page. People can get ready to do their part to close the gap between where the system is now and where they want it to be.

SHARED **measurement values both qualitative and quantitative data.**

SYSTEMS THINKERS ANALYZE progress on many parallel timelines. They look for both intended and unintended consequences of actions and track performance considering the system's real purpose. David Peter Stroh gave the example of shelter beds in homeless shelters to illustrate shared measurement. With systems thinking metrics, our main goal is to eradicate homelessness by focusing on having fewer shelter beds (short-term solution) and having more permanent housing (long-term solution). Conventional metrics concentrate on having more beds to receive more homeless in immediate need. [6]

CONTINUOUS COMMUNICATION IS key to the success of a collective impact. The quality and the consistency of the communication evolve as people get more attached to the common cause. They will also be able to better distinguish short-term fixes from long-term achievements. Communication by itself is not enough. It is essential to update information continuously as the cause evolves so that the communication can be up to date and relevant.

TELLING **system stories and the iceberg model.**

STORYTELLING IS a helpful tool to make sense of the world and how we fit in it. Stories are a way to share our experiences with others, let them know who we are and what is important to us. Stories can also be a compelling way to motivate and inspire others and make our message memorable. Storytelling has been used to help people suffering from traumatic events heal, to help keep the peace between groups humanizing the "enemy," allow politicians to connect with voters, and teachers to engage students in the learning material.

TO TELL A SYSTEM STORY, there must be some transformations in the way people think:

•Their view expands from just seeing their part of the system to seeing more of the system. They understand how and why the system is currently operating and what the plan is to change it.

•They move from blaming others and outside forces to accepting personal responsibility for their contribution to the problem and committing to change their behavior to help improve the system.

•They shift their focus from quickly reacting to immediate problems (school shooting, low-performing stock market) to directing their attention toward understanding the deeper system structures that cause those events to happen.

A SYSTEM STORY INCREASES SELF-AWARENESS. It opens people's eyes to how their actions may have had unintended consequences that contributed to their own problems and those of the system. It makes them more proactive. They realize that they already have the power and leverage to affect the desired change. They accept personal responsibility for their behavior and embrace their ability to create the change they want.

THE ICEBERG MODEL.

On its tragically ill-fated journey, the Titanic could have weathered the crash if it were not for the terrible damage caused by the massive portion of the iceberg lying beneath the surface.

THE SAME HAPPENS when we face a problem. When first looking at a problem, the concern and immediate focus may be on the tip of the iceberg: the event.

WE TRY to figure out what happened. We have the impulse to react quickly to put the fire out. But if we want to address more than the symptoms, and get to the root cause of the problem, reacting won't do it. We need to dig deep into where the real issues reside.

THE ICEBERG
A Toll for Guiding Systemic Thinking

EVENTS ———————————————— REACT
What just happened?
Catching a cold.

PATTERNS/TRENDS ————————— ANTICIPATE
What trends have there been over time?
I've been catching more colds
when sleeping less.

UNDERLYING STRUCTURES ————— DESIGN
What has influenced the patterns?
What are the relationships between the parts?
More stress at work, not eating well, difficulty
accessing healthy food near home or work.

MENTAL MODELS ———————————TRANSFORM
What assumptions, beliefs and values do people hold
about the system? What beliefs keep the system in place?
Career is the most important piece of our identity,
healthy food is too expensive, rest is for the unmotivated.

Diagram 17: The Iceberg Model[7]

THE ICEBERG MODEL distinguishes the symptoms and the real problems exposing the underlining structures of the system. The structure is where you will find the policies, dynamics of power, perceptions, and purpose. If left unchanged, the structure is where the vast majority of damage will come from as the trends and events will continue to repeat. The deeper your understanding of the system's structure, the more likely you will be to change the system's behavior for the long-term.

LET'S talk about the levels of the iceberg you can see in Diagram 17.

1. The Event Level

People perceive the world at the event level most of the time. For example, waking up in the middle of the night realizing that you're thirsty is an event level analysis. Event level problems can often be solved with a simple correction, like drinking a glass of water. However, the iceberg model encourages us to dig deeper instead of automatically assuming that the problem we face is indeed an event level one. Instead of just reacting to our thirst, let's dig deeper.

2. The Pattern Level

When we look beyond events, we can identify patterns. Events with strong resemblance have been occurring with us over time – we have been very thirsty in differing parts of the day. Maybe we are dangerously dehydrated. Acknowledging patterns helps us forecast and forestall events.

3. The Structure Level

When we try to find the answer to the question, "What's the cause of the pattern we are observing?" we usually conclude that it's embedded in the structure. Because of our increased workload in the heat of the day, we often forget to drink enough water. This has taken its toll on our bodies in the summer heat. Professor John Gerber informs us that structures can include the following things:

- Physical things — stores, sidewalks, or benches in a park.

- Organizations — corporations, hospitals, and schools.

- Policies — regulations, restrictions, or taxes.

- Rituals — subconscious behaviors. [8]

4. The Mental Model Level

The fourth level of the iceberg is mental models. These are the attitudes, beliefs, expectations, morals, and values that provide the structure a reason to function. For example, the beliefs we subconsciously adopt from our home or from school, work, and surroundings. In the case of our dehydration, the mental model we create could involve the belief that our job is more important than our health. Or that by taking a short drinking break, we might appear lazy. [9]

LET'S carry our iceberg analogy to a specific example of a systemic problem: the reform of the justice system affecting incarceration rates. Between 1960 and 2008, incarceration levels rose by 60% despite a

25% drop in crimes committed. Some people argued that this data showed that locking people up for committing crimes resulted in the overall crime rate dropping. Others thought racism and fear were driving more incarcerations rather than the serious-ness of the crime committed.

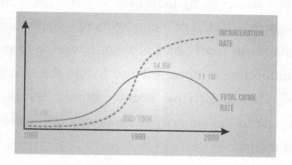

DIAGRAM 18: Crime Rates Versus Incarceration Rates.

Reforming the criminal justice system is a complex task. We won't find solutions at the tip of the iceberg. Being most concerned with the latest statistics on crimes committed, repeat offenders, and the prison system's costs, analysts miss the big picture.

The typical, well-intentioned "solution" is issuing harsh sentences to those who commit crimes. But no one seems concerned with the reintegration of people who have been incarcerated into society. After people are released from prison, their criminal record discourages future employment opportunities. These men and women have been emotionally and psychologically hardened by their time in jail. That, coupled with their lack of employment opportunities, contributes to nearly half of them returning to prison for committing a repeat offense within the first three years. The underlying socioeconomic issues that contribute to the majority of inner-city crime are also out of focus.

The sentences don't address the vacuum left in the communities, increasing the likelihood of future generations committing crimes, the lack of high-quality foster care. No one is improving the high recidivism rate due to a lack of unpreparedness of ex-convicts. Prisons don't actually reform criminals. Most imprisoned people need education, marketable skills. If, as a society, we punish them for the crime they commit in perpetuity, why would we expect them to change? Of course, some crimes are harder to forgive than others. And without true repentance, it is almost impossible to trust someone who committed criminal acts. [10]

Some countries don't impose the death penalty or life sentences, even for the harshest crimes. Let's take Norway as an example. The now forty-one-year-old Anders Behring Breivick murdered seventy-seven people (including children) in 2011. He was sentenced to twenty-one years in prison, which may be prolonged if deemed required. He lives in conditions described as "a three-room suite with windows, about 340 square feet, including a treadmill, a fridge, a DVD player, a Sony PlayStation, and a desk with a typewriter. He has been taking distance-learning courses at his country's main university. He has access to television, radio, and newspapers. He prepares his own food, and he entered the Christmas gingerbread-house baking contest at his prison." [11]

While the case of Andres Behring Breivick is extreme, and clearly shows the unpreparedness of the Norwegian legal system to punish the crimes as he committed, the inmates of Norway do have a mentality that they will go back into society, and reintegrate. They have this mindset because the incarceration in Norway's criminal justice system works on the principle of restorative justice and rehabilitating prisoners. There are correctional facilities, which make sure that prisoners can become productive and helpful members of society again. This approach helps Norway maintain one of the lowest recidivism rates globally, currently twenty percent, with less than 4000 people in prison and one of the world's lowest crime rates. [121314]

The story of balancing feedback loops.

Balancing feedback loops are the driving force behind improving a social system because they act to correct behavior by closing the gap between where the system currently is and where we want it to be.

When a balancing feedback loop is achieving its purpose, the corrections it makes can be nearly undetectable, and we tend to take it for granted. When the balancing loop is underperforming, we become aware of it. Balancing feedback loops can reveal why the system is resistant to change.

Corrective action fails to work for one or more of the following reasons:

•As soon as we think the problem is solved, we stop focusing on the solution and open the door for the issue to come back. An example of this was demonstrated in Boston in the early 1990s. Boston administrators were trying to solve the problem of youth crime in the city. Community and political leaders coordinated their efforts to solve the problem. They came up with various solutions like after-school programs, community policing, neighborhood watches, and gang outreach, all of which proved to be very successful in reducing youth crime. Thinking that the problem was solved, the political leaders removed funding from these programs to address other concerns. It wasn't long before the issue of youth crime returned. [15]

•We underestimate the amount of time it will take to effect positive lasting change. When change doesn't happen on our schedule, we can get discouraged and give up too soon. Or get impatient and push too hard for results before they are ready. Thankfully, a community in Massachusetts was more patient and persistent than most. They were experiencing a problem with high rates of teen and adult drug and alcohol abuse. The community remained committed to their coordinated efforts. After eleven years, they experienced success with their solution for bringing the teen alcohol and drug abuse rates down.

•The system participants are not unified behind a clear-shared vision and purpose. They disagree on a shared understanding of where the system currently is and where it should be. Without a common plan, there is little hope for coming up with a solution that will bring meaningful and lasting change.

Based on the observations made in the three points above, policy makers can adjust their actions as follows:

-Ensure the reinforcement of the interventions that prove to bring good results instead of reducing support when the problem becomes less pressing.

-Acknowledge the perception, delivery, and adoption delay of the correcting actions. Practice patience and persistence with the interference.

-Before developing an intervention strategy, make sure every actor involved shares the same understanding, goals, and reality.

The story of reinforcing feedback loops: success to the successful.

In the systems archetypes chapter, the "success to the successful" archetype has a reinforcing feedback loop in control. Let's recapitulate the main system story behind this archetype:

- Systems have a finite amount of resources. When one person or group gains an advantage over another in terms of wealth or success, they can use it to gain even more resources. This is not a bad thing by itself, but it may put the other person or group at a disadvantage of allocating resources. This disadvantage grows as time passes because they cannot get the resources they need to stay competitive. The gap widens over time, and it becomes a complex cycle to break.

- Those who are wealthy have more money to invest in land, equipment, stocks and bonds, and better education and healthcare. This, in turn, makes them better able to earn more income and accumulate more wealth. Their capital allows them to be more productive. The wealthy also have more access to other influential people who can offer them better networking and business opportunities that contribute to their success.

- Those who are not wealthy have to spend more of their money on goods. They don't have money to invest and generate more wealth. The gap between the haves and have nots continues to widen, and the cycle keeps repeating.

In a social system, reinforcing loops create dynamics that support the majority of wealth and success to concentrate in the hands of a few. Other dynamics line up against the lower class, especially minorities, to experience comparable levels of success. Keith Lawrence, the co-director of Aspen Institute Round-table on Community Change, calls this phenomenon structural racism. He argues that some dynamics – historical, cultural, institutional, and interpersonal - regularly favor white people and exponentially hinder the chances of people of color to succeed. He strengthens his statement by bringing up examples such as gerrymandering. The fact that the majority of incarcerated people are black men. [16] Children born into less fortunate families start their lives off at a disadvantage. Their parents are under tremendous pressure to make ends meet and may not afford high-quality health care.

Societies whose main aim is to sustainability mini-mize the "success to the successful" archetype and improve their redistribution system. They also raise awareness of the structural problems of resource allo-cations.

9

A Comprehensive Study on Systems Thinking and a Social Issue

The story.

Calhoun County, Michigan, around Battle Creek, with a population of about 100,000, had a chronic social problem of homelessness. Business, political, and community leaders, along with the homeless, began asking questions about why, despite their best efforts, they were still unable to end homelessness in their community. They united with the Battle Creek Homeless Coalition, determined to find a solution of positive lasting change. They combined their efforts and used systems thinking to gather behind a purpose and common agenda to create a ten-year plan to eliminate homelessness in their area. They studied data and worked to form a shared vision of where they want to be and an honest picture and understanding of where they currently were. They agreed upon the leverage points that they thought would be most effective and helpful in redesigning the system's structure. [1]

THEY DID a thorough research about the risk factors of homelessness, the four stages of homelessness. Why people end up on the streets only temporarily? By conducting many interviews with people in their community, they identified a major concern—the difficulty of moving people from temporary homeless shelters into safe, affordable, supportive, permanent housing.

HOMELESSNESS HAS FOUR STAGES:

-"People becoming at risk of losing their homes.

-People losing their homes and having to live on the streets.

-People finding temporary shelter off the streets.

-People moving from temporary shelter back into permanent housing." [2]

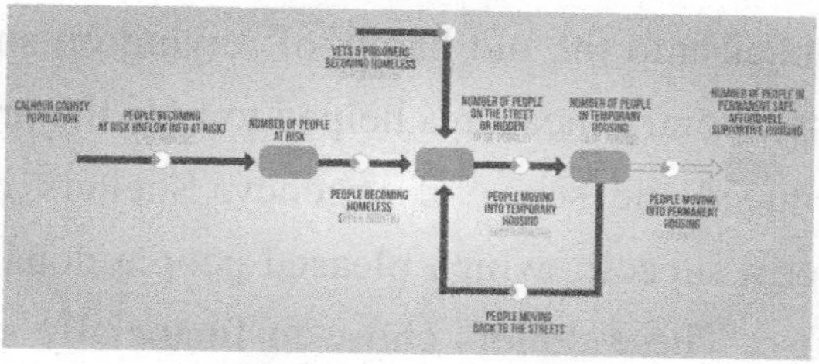

DIAGRAM 19: The Four Stages Of Homelessness.[3]

THE BATTLE CREEK Homeless Coalition took steps towards success:

- providing government subsidies to help keep people in their own homes;

- getting the entire community – schools, churches, families, and friends – involved in offering their support,

- informing people of the community assistance and programs that were available to them,

- and enlisting the help of the Veteran's Administration to offer help to veterans.

THESE WERE all good steps but not enough to sustain the solution in the long run. They didn't want to fall back into the old habits of relying on shelters. These temporary measures helped to hide the problem and reduced the sense of urgency. Shelters offered short-term success, which pleased people donating to the cause. These donors chose to financially support individual organizations, completely shifting shelters' focus from the big picture and competing for resources instead.

THE QUICK FIX of supporting shelters addressed a symptom. It didn't get to the root of the problem of homelessness. It caused unintended negative consequences as shelters created dependence.

THE BATTLE CREEK Homeless Coalition identified seven leverage points that they felt would give them the most "bang for their buck" in changing the system as a whole. They grouped them according to whether they were designed to reduce the inflow into shelters - by keeping people at risk of becoming homeless. Or increase the outflow by getting more people to move out of the temporary shelters into permanent housing.

. . .

AFTER ALL OF their intensive study, they found that the cheapest leverage points to implement were those that kept people in their own homes and prevented them from becoming homeless in the first place. They coordinated their efforts to increase affordable housing by supporting landlords who were willing to rent to people at risk. They tried to create additional better-paying jobs so that people at risk could afford their rent payments. They also provided integrated community services designed to give people the support they needed to stay in their homes. [4]

RESULTS

Were their efforts successful? During the first three years of implementing their plan, from 2007-2009, homelessness decreased by 13%, and eviction rates dropped by 3%. This was despite the recession our country was in that spurred a 70% increase in unemployment and a 15% increase in people filing for bankruptcy in Calhoun County. [5]

. . .

THE COORDINATING COUNCIL of Calhoun County reported that in 2016, 1,190 people were considered "literally homeless." This means that they were either living in a public or private shelter or in a public or private place not intended for human habitation. Based on this data and the county's new regulations, they are on track to potentially reduce homelessness by 28% in 9 years. System changes don't happen overnight, but the fact that homelessness is on the decline by a significant percentage in Calhoun County is promising progress. [6]

THE FOUR STAGES **of change based on the homeless story.**

AUTHOR DAVID PETER STROH identifies four stages of change. Stroh, quoting Peter Sange, the author of the book The Fifth Discipline, describes social changes as such, "the energy for change is mobilized by establishing a discrepancy between what people want and where they are. (…) When people have a common aspiration – as expressed by a shared vision, mission, and set of values – and a shared understanding of not only where they are now but also why – then they establish creative tension, which they are drawn to resolve in favor of their aspiration." [7]

CREATING A SHARED understanding is crucial to see why the current problems exist and the best solutions. For example, they will know how the pressure to build a new homeless shelter is only a band-aid to the problem. Homelessness will persist, and so will their dependence on the shelters.

THE SHARED picture will help people to commit to the idea "I will get my part done, and I'll make sure we all get the whole thing done." The creative tension rooting in the shared picture brings forth the idea of the four stages of change. Let's go through these stages one by one.

1.STAGE 1 – This is where the foundation of the change is built. In the case of our story, stage one occurred when the Battle Creek Homeless Coalition and the homeless people asked for the input of business, political, and community leaders of Calhoun

County. They met and started asking hard questions about why they still had a homelessness problem despite their best efforts. They decided that they were ready to make a change. These stakeholders were actively engaged in coming up with a common agenda. They agreed upon where they would like for the system to be. They cultivated a shared vision of what successful change would look like and set their common purpose. They learned how to effectively communicate with each other.

2.STAGE 2 – This is the "reality check" stage. The Coalition gathered and organized information to give a clear and honest picture of where the system was currently. They did interviews and looked back in history to see if the system had been there before. Then they organized the information they had gathered to develop a basic system analysis. They checked how people interacted before to help or deter the common goal. They formed a shared view of what was happening and began to analyze why it was happening. They accepted responsibility for any role they may have played in contributing to the problem.

. . .

3.STAGE 3 – This is a "tell it like it is" stage. At this stage, people have to face the fact that change is hard and things might have to get worse before they get better. In this stage, they acknowledge that even in a flawed system, there is some benefit that people are getting. Or the system wouldn't be stuck where it was.

REAL AND LASTING change takes a significant investment of time, effort, money, and resources. It requires commitment and sacrifice on the part of everyone involved.

THIS STAGE IS where people recognize that they will need to resist the temptation of giving in to quick fixes and short-term solutions and stick with the plan for the long haul. They have to weigh the benefits and sacrifices that will accompany change and the costs of not acting. Hard trade-offs, delayed gratification, temporary back fall should all be accepted side effects of the change. They need to make a conscious choice to buy in fully to the purpose and commit to being part of the solution.

. . .

IN OUR STORY, this was where the Battle Creek Homeless Coalition reached a crucial turning point in developing a solution. They realized the system was currently helping people cope with homelessness by providing them with shelters. But that was ultimately undermining the purpose of ending homelessness.

4.STAGE 4 — This is where people bridge the gap between where the system currently is and where they want it to be. In this stage, they identify the leverage points they believe will be most helpful in creating change. They commit to continuous learning and agree to meet to update and adjust their plan and goals to stay on track of achieving the unified purpose.

IN THE CASE of our story, the leverage points the Coalition selected served as the goals for their ten-year plan. When they began to get a hold of what was working and identified needs that others could help meet, they reached out to bring in and engage new stakeholders. They brought in people who could help with economic development in creating new better paying jobs. People with ideas and resources for increasing affordable housing. And people with experience in foster care and the criminal justice system.

THESE STAGES WORK in a circular process. What we learned in Stage 4 gives feedback to Stage 1, and the cycle continues.

10

Exercises

This chapter will lay out some exercises that can be helpful for team building. Get your systems thinking juices flowing. Begin to work on analyzing a system's problems and generating a lasting and meaningful solution.

A WARM UP exercise

THIS ICEBREAKER IS an excellent way to start a meeting where the goal is to challenge people's creativity and inner idea machine.

. . .

TIME:

About 5 minutes.

INSTRUCTIONS:

Explain this as an exercise to practice mental agility before beginning the meeting. Ask participants to follow your instructions mentally. Speak slowly and pause between each instruction:

1) choose a number from 1 to 9

2) subtract 5

3) multiply it by 3

4) square the number (multiply by the same number-- not square root)

5) add the digits together until you get only one digit (i.e. 64=6+4= 10 = 1+0=1)

6) if the number is less than 5, add five - otherwise subtract 4.

7) multiply it by 2

8) subtract 6

9) match the digit to a letter in the alphabet 1=A, 2=B, 3=C, etc...

10) choose the name of a country that begins with that letter

11) take the second letter in the country's name and think of an animal that begins with that letter

12) think of the color of that animal

RESULTS:

Chances are you thought of a grey or pink elephant from Denmark.

WHY?

THE NUMBER TRICK GIVES YOU A "4" every time, which means you always think of a "D." The countries that start with the letter "D" are Denmark, Djibouti, and the Dominican Republic. Djibouti deserves a 1% chance if you happen to come from there or the area. So does the Dominican Republic.

But let's be honest, it's not surprising that most people think of Denmark.

WHAT IF WE indeed picked Djibouti? We'd get animals like jaguars, jackals, jackrabbits, or jellyfish. If we picked Dominican Republic, we'd come up with an octopus, otter, owl, ostrich, or one of many other possibilities. Since we chose Denmark, our animal name had to begin with an "e." If you chose elephant, you picked the most common answer, and likely the first one popped into your head.

KEEP in mind when we are content to pick the quick and/or popular answer that means most other people, including our competitors, are coming up with the same answer too. Let's spend time looking for something beyond the most obvious thought. Here are some animals that begin with the letter "e:"

-eagles

-earless seals

-earthworms

-earwigs

-echidnas

-elephant beetles

-emperor moths

-emperor penguins

-emydid turtles

-engraver beetles

-ensign wasp.

Do you have any questions left?

PLAYING **and Designing a Game**

Choose a well-known board game. Review the rules of the game with the participants, and then decide to change the rules. Ask each person in your group to change one of the rules by changing, adding, or eliminating one of the original rules. Play the new version of the game created collectively by the group. Ask the following questions for discussion:

· · ·

1. What does having a set of rules tell us about how a system works?

2. What's the difference between playing and designing a game?

3. What is different about the system when the game is being played and when it is being designed?

RESULTS:

This activity is presented in a fun game format. Still, it provides a good opportunity to compare and contrast playing and designing. When we play a game, our focus is on taking turns as we follow the rules laid out for us and try to win. In contrast, designing the game involves not only playing it but also requires a higher level of thinking skill. You need to reflect upon the possible changes you might make and the consequences resulting from those changes.

DESIGNING REQUIRES an understanding of the holistic and systemic view of the game. When you design a game, you make decisions based on who the target audience is. That's why we have different games and different rules. We use the same tools tailored for different people, such as children, and different purposes, such as whether it is intended to teach a skill or it is just to be played for fun. We can discover the rules and variations through repeated occasions of playing the same game. From experiences like these, we can gain a deeper understanding of the meaning of being part of a system..[1]

From *Seven Activities to Engage Systems Thinking* by Arne Collen & Gianfranco Minati

A LANGUAGE GAME

This game is best played with another person whose primary language is your secondary language. Choose a word or phrase from your primary language and translate it into your secondary language. For example, if English is your primary language, you might translate the words into Spanish. You would then ask the person you are playing with to translate the Spanish back into English. Continue taking turns back and forth until each person has completed several words or phrases. Observe the differences in meaning between the original words of the primary speaker and those translated back in a secondary language. Ask the following questions for discussion:

1.HOW IS language important in a living system?

2.What can happen when two systems, that have different languages, must communicate?

3.What problems can arise when two systems with different languages try to communicate?

4.What solutions might help address the problems that can arise when two systems with different languages need to communicate?

THERE IS a move to help people communicate across different languages by using Artificial Intelligence. This can solve some communication problems, but there is also the potential for some meaning to be lost by having a computer translate. To avoid this, there is a recognition that translation does require input from a human being. Translations always have an author and are copyrighted. As we become more connected in our world, our extensive global communications network has become a system of its own. It is interconnected and interdependent with language subsystems. We need to be respectful, tolerant, and appreciative of diversity. We should be open to the possibility of learning from language and cultures that are quite different from our own and be kind and ethical global citizens.[2]

From *Seven Activities to Engage Systems Thinking* by Arne Collen & Gianfranco Minati

SPOT

This exercise works best with groups of less than ten people. Some people will not fall into the trap, but most will. The idea is not to trick or embarrass people but rather to get everyone laughing together. This can spark discussions about the power of mindfulness and how it helps us think systemically.

TIME:

About 5 minutes.

INSTRUCTIONS:

Quickly ask an individual or small group the following questions. Only pause briefly to allow a response and ask them to answer in a loud, energetic voice:

1.Ask them to say the word SPOT three times as quickly as they can

2.Ask them to spell the word SPOT once

3.Now, ask them what they do when they come to a green light.

RESULTS:

Many people will say STOP, a few will say GO. If you ask them the question again, many will repeat the same answer and possibly get defensive about their answer being right.

YOU COULD THEN ASK THEM, "How many of you drove to work today? What did you do when you came to a green light?" Joke that you could've asked them what they do when they get to red light. You suspect that if they're anything like many other drivers in your town, they would probably run through it.

WE LIVE in a society that often expects people to give answers as quickly as possible. There is comfort in numbers, so when we hear others saying the same answer we are giving, we feel more confident that we are right. While it is good to allow ourselves to fall into patterns (they are healthy signs), sometimes we need to slow down and check our answers to be sure we are giving the correct ones.[3]

From *The Systems Thinking Playbook* by Linda Booth Sweeney & Dennis Meadows

Simon Says

This exercise can allow the group to walk around a little and stretch after a long period of sitting. Or to serve as a fun and gentle reminder that we can all benefit from listening a little more carefully.

TIME:

About 5 minutes.

INSTRUCTIONS:

Introduce this activity as a chance for the participants to experience the latest test that the police are giving when they pull drivers over to check for drinking and driving.

1. Stand up, get in front of the participants and ask them to stand up too. Explain to them that in this activity, they have to do what you tell them to do.

2. Ask them to stretch both of their arms out at shoulder height (as you say it do it as well)

3. Ask them to make a circle with the thumb and index finger of their right hand (you do it as you are saying it)

4. Ask them to take their thumb and index finger (still in the circle), and put the circle on their cheek (you will put your thumb and index finger on your chin instead)

RESULTS:

Most people will have put their thumb and index finger on their chin instead of on their cheek because most people will have followed your actions instead of your words.

IT IS important that we follow through with our actions to support what we have said we will do.[4]

FROM *THE SYSTEMS Thinking Playbook* by Linda Booth Sweeney & Dennis Meadows

Afterword

Systems thinking is a powerful lens through which we can analyze the world. It impacts our ability to make well-informed objective decisions based on evidence and data. With systems thinking, we can get to the root cause of even the most challenging, complex, and chronic problems. We can create a strategic plan of the highest quality that aligns everyone's efforts on the system's unifying purpose.

Here is a short compilation of things we can accomplish by using systems thinking:

•See the big picture (the whole system) more clearly.

•Discover and accept responsibility for the unintended negative consequences that we may have inadvertently caused through our actions.

•Develop solutions that are beneficial to the entire system and create lasting and meaningful changes.

•Avoid quick fixes that ultimately can make things worse in the long term.

•Increase our understanding of the problems we are trying to solve.

•Leverage points that make the best possible use of available resources.

•View learning as a worthwhile and continuous process.

•Commit to doing your part to improve the entire system.

•Recognize that our individual and collective thinking impacts the results we achieve.

Systems thinking is a paradigm shift. We move from blaming people and things we can't control to accepting responsibility and empowering ourselves to take control of our own reality. It is a shift from being emotionally attached to our own beliefs to being humble and open to others' ideas and opinions. It involves accepting that we aren't always right and that we have plenty to learn from others.

The core principles of how systems work:

•Feedback: the way a system performs is closely tied to the circular, interconnected relationships within it.

•Growth & Stability: Feedback loops show us how systems grow (reinforcing loops) or remain stable (equilibrium caused by balancing loops).

•Diversity & Resilience: Diversity allows systems to grow while resilience keeps systems stable when change occurs.

•Delay: Our choices and actions result in consequences that can be immediate or delayed.

•Power of Awareness: When we take a good, hard, honest look at where a system is currently operating, we can build upon its strengths and work to overcome its weaknesses.

•Unintended Consequences: The challenges we are facing today may result from a solution we instituted in the past.

•Leverage: Meaningful and lasting change within a system occurs when we focus on implementing a few coordinated changes and sustaining them over time.

Understanding these core principles is key to recognizing patterns in system behavior to create a strategic plan aimed at achieving the system's purpose.

Donella Meadows explained, "Social systems are the external manifestations of cultural thinking patterns and of profound human needs, emotions, strengths, and weaknesses." [1] To be effective in bringing about social change, we have to strengthen our systems thinking skills.

While we often think of our cognitive abilities as the key to systems thinking, strong systems thinkers also develop themselves in emotional, behavioral, physical, and spiritual areas. Being well-rounded in all areas of life makes us better prepared and more efficient in facing the challenges we wish to overcome.

Becoming a systems thinker takes practice. There will be times when you will need to seek guidance and help from others - when you get stuck because the task seems impossible. It is then that you should rely on one of the most critical skills systems thinkers have – the ability to ask great questions. When we ask the right questions, we open ourselves to new ways of thinking, communicating, and understanding. Here are examples of a few powerful questions:

•Why are we unable to achieve our goal despite our best efforts and intentions?

•What responsibility do we bear for the problems we are facing?

•How can we create common ground among our stakeholders?

•What sacrifices will we need to make to enable the system as a whole to succeed?

•What might the unintended consequences of this possible solution be?

Systems thinkers need to view themselves as works in progress. There is always new knowledge to be gained and always room to learn, grow, and improve. Some characteristics are helpful to cultivate within ourselves; these are curiosity, respect, and compassion. [2]

Systems thinking gives us the tools and skills we need to take a complex, and sometimes chronic problem, improve our shared understanding of it, and align and organize the pieces into a clear roadmap. Pave the path we should take to redesign the system's structure and achieve its purpose.

Systems thinking is about connections: making, recognizing, understanding, and strengthening them. Everything in a system is connected. We need to cultivate and nurture positive relationships and diminish or remove the dysfunctional ones. It isn't long until we have the system elements working together in harmony, united in service to the whole. Try to contribute to the greater good. What could be better than that?

A.R.

Reference

Books and printed papers:

Beresford-Jones, D., S. Arce, O.Q. Whaley and A. Chepstow-Lusty. The Role of Prosopis in Ecological and Landscape Change in the Samaca Basin, Lower Ica Valley, South Coast Peru from the Early Horizon to the Late Intermediate Period. Latin American Antiquity Vol. 20 pp. 303–330. 2009.

Booth Sweeney, Linda. Meadows, Dennis. The Systems Thinking Playbook. Chelsea Green Publishing. 2010.

Forrester, Jay. Collected Papers of Jay Forrester. Jay Forrester. Pegasus Communications. 1975.

Frey, Rebecca Joyce. Genocide and International Justice. Facts On File. ISBN 978-0816073108. 2009.

Geoff W Adams, The Emperor Commodus : gladiator, Hercules or a tyrant?. Boca Raton: BrownWalker Press. ISBN 1612337228. 2013.

Meadows, Donella. Thinking in Systems: A primer. Chelsea Green Publishing. 2008.

Seonmin Kim, Victoria Jane Mabin, John Davies. The theory of constraints thinking processes: retrospect and prospect. International Journal of Operations & Production Management, Vol. 28 Issue: 2, pp.155-184. 2008. https://doi.org/10.1108/01443570810846883

Silverman Helaine. Proulx ,Donald A. The Nasca. Blackwell Publishers. Malden. 2002.

Stroh, Peter David. Systems Thinking For Social Change. Chelsea Green Publishing. 2015.

Von Bertalanffy, Ludwig. An Outline of General System Theory. The British Journal for the Philosophy of Science, Vol. 1, No. 2, pp. 134-165. 1950.

Online Articles and studies:

Aronson, Daniel. Overview of Systems Thinking. Daniel Aronson. 1996. http://www.thinking.net/Systems_Thinking/OverviewSTarticle.pdf

Battle Creek Michigan. Homeless Coalition discusses local facts on health fair day. Battle Creek Michigan. 2017. https://www.battlecreekmi.gov/CivicAlerts.aspx?AID=505&ARC=624

Beattie, Andrwe. Why Buying in Bulk Doesn't Always Save You Money. Investopedia. 2018. https://www.investopedia.com/articles/pf/07/bulk_buying.asp

Bregel, Emily. Fog-induced wreck prompted lawsuits. Times Free Press. 2010. https://www.timesfreepress.com/news/news/story/2010/dec/05/fog-induced-wreck-prompted-lawsuits/36307/

Chatteerjee, Pratap. Dick Cheney's Halliburton: a corporate case study. The Guardian. 2011. https://www.theguardian.com/commentisfree/cifamerica/2011/jun/08/dick-cheney-halliburton-supreme-court

Collaboration for Impact. The Collective Impact Framework. Collaboration for Impact. 2018.

Collen, Arne. Minati, Gianfranco. Seven Activities To Engage Systems Thinking. Semantic Scholar. 1997.

https://pdfs.semanticscholar.org/3436/
c52688ab6dae545fdb783bb0b88b8b052c16.pdf

Darling-Hammond, Linda. Inequality in Teaching and Schooling: How Opportunity Is Rationed to Students of Color in America NCBI. 2001. https://www.ncbi.nlm.nih.gov/books/NBK223640/

Death Penalty Information Center. Deterrence: States Without the Death Penalty Have Had Consistently Lower Murder Rates. Death Penalty Information Center. 2017. https://deathpenaltyinfo.org/deterrence-states-without-death-penalty-have-had-consistently-lower-murder-rates

Durose, Matthew. Cooper, Alexia D. Ph.D., Snyder, Howard N. Ph.D. Recidivism of Prisoners Released in 30 States in 2005: Patterns from 2005 to 2010. U.S. Department of Justice. 2014. https://www.bjs.gov/content/pub/pdf/rprts05p0510.pdf

Gav, Big. Norman Borlaug: Saint Or Sinner? Resilience. 2009. https://www.resilience.org/stories/2009-10-01/norman-borlaug-saint-or-sinner/

Gerber, John. Systems Thinking Tools: Finding The Root Cause(S) Of Big Problems. Changing The Story.

2012.   https://changingthestory.net/2012/07/18/
rootcaus/

Hale, David M. Behind the bling: The story of Clemson's epic championship rings. ESPN. 2017. http://www.espn.com/college-football/story/_/id/20466841/clemson-tigers-dabo-swinney-big-business-college-football-championship-rings

Herbert, Christopher E. Haurin , Donald R. Rosenthal, Stuart S. Duda, Mark. Homeownership Gaps Among Low-Income and Minority Borrowers and Neighborhoods. U.S. Department of Housing and Urban Development. 2005. https://www.huduser.gov/Publications/pdf/HomeownershipGapsAmongLow-IncomeAndMinority.pdf

Integrated Taxonomy Information System. https://www.itis.gov

Invasive Animals CRC. Introduction of the cane toad to Australia. Pest Smart. 2012. https://www.pestsmart.org.au/pestsmart-case-study-introduction-of-the-cane-toad-to-australia/

I See Systems. Applying Systems Thinking and Common Archetypes to Organizational Issues. Module 6: Systems Archetypes. 2018. https://www.

iseesystems.com/Online_training/course/module6/6-02-0-0-what.htm

I See Systems. Original picture from Applying Systems Thinking and Common Archetypes to Organizational Issues. Module 6: Systems Archetypes. Implications & Leverage Points. Escalation. I See Systems. 2018. https://www.iseesystems.com/Online_training/course/module6/6-11-3-0-escalimp.htm

I See Systems. Applying Systems Thinking and Common Archetypes to Organizational Issues. Module 6: Systems Archetypes. Implications & Leverage Points. Shifting the Burden. I See Systems. 2018. https://www.iseesystems.com/Online_training/course/module6/6-06-3-0-shiftimp.htm

I See Systems. Applying Systems Thinking and Common Archetypes to Organizational Issues. Module 6: Systems Archetypes. Implications & Leverage Points. Success to the Successful. I See Systems. 2018. https://www.iseesystems.com/Online_training/course/module6/6-13-3-0-successimp.htm

Johnston, Ian. Pesticides linked to 'large-scale population extinctions' of wild beesIndependent. 2016. https://www.independent.co.uk/news/science/insecti

cides-bees-population-extinction-link-farmers-toxic-neonicotinoid-oilseed-rape-a7193951.html

Karash, Richard. Mental Models And Systems Thinking: Going Deeper Into Systemic Issues. The Systems Thinker. 2018. https://thesystemsthinker.com/mental-models-and-systems-thinking-going-deeper-into-systemic-issues/

Karash, Richard. Goodman, Michael R. Going Deeper: Moving from Understanding to Action. Applied Systems Thinking. 1995.

http://www.appliedsystemsthinking.com/supporting_documents/PracticeGoingDeeper.pdf

Kubish C, Anne. Structural Racism. Racial Equity Tools. 2006. www.racialequitytools.org/resource-files/kubisch.pdf [URL inactive]

Kushinka, Matthew. Countries That Start with D: There's Something Rotten in America. Red Lines. 2018. https://www.redlinels.com/countries-start-d/

Lynn, Bryan. Many US States Struggle with Teacher Shortages. Learning English. 2018. https://learningenglish.voanews.com/a/many-us-states-struggle-with-teacher-shortages/4537983.html

Martin, Will. The 31 safest countries in the world. Business Insider. 2018. https://www.businessinsider. my/safest-countries-in-the-world-2018-6/?r= US&IR=T

Merritt, Jeremy. What Are Mental Models? The Systems Thinker. 2018. https://thesystemsthinker. com/what-are-mental-models/

Newswire. Ramapough Mountain Indians Sue Ford Over Toxic Contamination. Newswire. 2006. http:// www.ens-newswire.com/ens/jan2006/2006-01-21-01.html

Northwest Earth Institute. A Systems Thinking Model: The Iceberg. Northwest Earth Institute. 2018. https://www.nwei.org/iceberg/

Onda, Tsuyoshi. Abortion Worldwide 2017: Uneven Progress and Unequal Access. Guttmacher. 2018. https://www.guttmacher.org/report/abortion-world wide-2017

Pilkington, Ed. Robin Wright targets Congo's 'conflict minerals' violence with new campaign. The Guardian. 2016. https://www.theguardian.com/world/2016/may/ 17/robin-wright-stand-with-congo-campaign-mining-house-of-cards

Pryser Libell, Henrik. Anders Behring Breivik, Killer in 2011 Norway Massacre, Says Prison Conditions Violate His Rights. The New York Times. 2016. https://www.nytimes.com/2016/03/16/world/europe/anders-breivik-nazi-prison-lawsuit.html

Sherwell, Philip. A plague of Burmese pythons in the Everglades. The Telegraph. 2009. https://www.telegraph.co.uk/news/worldnews/northamerica/usa/5956739/A-plague-of-Burmese-pythons-in-the-Everglades.html

Sterbenz, Christina. Why Norway's prison system is so successful. Business Insider. 2014. https://www.businessinsider.com/why-norways-prison-system-is-so-successful-2014-12/?IR=T

Stroh, Peter David. Goodman, Michael. A Systemic Approach to Ending Homelessness. Applied Systems Thinking. 2007. http://www.appliedsystemsthinking.com/supporting_documents/TopicalHomelessness.pdf

Stover, Del. Addressing teacher turnover in high-poverty, high-minority urban schools. NSBA. 2017. https://www.nsba.org/newsroom/addressing-teacher-turnover-high-poverty-high-minority-urban-schools

Strachan, Glenn. Systems Thinking. International Research Institute in Sustainability, University of Gloucestershire. 2018. http://arts.brighton.ac.uk/__data/assets/pdf_file/0004/5926/Systems-Thinking.pdf

The Associated Press. Louisiana school has rescinded its hair extension ban after outcry, archdiocese says. CBC. 2018. https://www.cbc.ca/news/world/black-girl-hair-school-policy-extensions-1.4801371

The Nobel Prize. Norman E. Borlaug. The Nobel Prize. 2018. https://www.nobelprize.org/prizes/peace/1970/borlaug/symposia/

Volz, Matt. Fired pregnant teacher settles with Montana Catholic school. The Boston Globe. 2016. https://www.bostonglobe.com/news/nation/2016/03/15/fired-pregnant-teacher-settles-with-montana-catholic-school/ShlqaNHnaXXWO2HVUcDxiM/story.html

Von Bertalanffy, Ludwig. The Theory of Open Systems in Physics and Biology Science New Series, Vol. 111, No. 2872 (Jan. 13, 1950), pp. 23-29 Published by: American Association for the Advancement of Science Stable URL: https://www.jstor.org/stable/1676073

World Prison Brief. Highest to Lowest. Prison Population Total. World Prison Brief. 2018. http://www.prisonstudies.org/highest-to-lowest/prison-population-total?field_region_taxonomy_tid=All

Zurcher, Kathleen. Stroh, Peter David. Acting and Thinking Systemically. The Systems Thinker. 2018. https://thesystemsthinker.com/acting-and-thinking-systemically/

Notes

Introduction

1. The Nazca culture was an archaeological culture that thrived from c. 100 BC to 800 CE in the southern coast of Peru between the river valleys of Ica and the Rio Grande de Nazca drainage. The Nazca left behind a rich variety of crafts and technologies such as ceramics, textiles, and geoglyphs—today known as the Nazca Lines. They also built an imposing underground aqueduct system that still works today. Extracted from *The Nasca by Helaine Silverman and Donald A. Proulx. Blackwell Publishers. Malden. 2002.*

2. Silverman Helaine. Proulx ,Donald A. The Nasca. Blackwell Publishers. Malden. 2002.

3. Beresford-Jones, D., S. Arce, O.Q. Whaley and A. Chepstow-Lusty. The Role of Prosopis in Ecological and Landscape Change in the Samaca Basin, Lower Ica Valley, South Coast Peru from the Early Horizon to the Late Intermediate Period. Latin American Antiquity Vol. 20 pp. 303–330. 2009.

4. The Nobel Prize. Norman E. Borlaug. The Nobel Prize. 2018. https://www.nobelprize.org/prizes/peace/1970/borlaug/symposia/

5. Johnston, Ian. Pesticides linked to 'large-scale population extinctions' of wild beesIndependent. 2016. https://www.independent.co.uk/news/science/insecticides-bees-population-extinction-link-farmers-toxic-neonicotinoid-oilseed-rape-a7193951.html

6. Gav, Big. Norman Borlaug: Saint Or Sinner? Resilience. 2009. https://www.resilience.org/stories/2009-10-01/norman-borlaug-saint-or-sinner/

1. Where Is Systems Thinking Coming From?

1. Von Bertalanffy, Ludwig. An Outline of General System Theory. The British Journal for the Philosophy of Science, Vol. 1, No. 2, pp. 134-165. 1950.
2. A direct translation of isomorphic means literally "same form."
3. "The principle that growth or decay of some physical quantity is at a rate such that its value at a certain time or place is the initial value times e raised to a power equal to a constant times some convenient coordinate, such as the elapsed time or the distance traveled by a wave; there is growth if the constant is positive, decay if it is negative." *From McGraw-Hill Dictionary of Scientific & Technical Terms, 6E. S.v. "exponential law." Retrieved August 9 2018 from https://encyclopedia2. thefreedictionary.com/exponential+law*
4. Von Bertalanffy, Ludwig. An Outline of General System Theory. The British Journal for the Philosophy of Science, Vol. 1, No. 2, pp. 134-165. 1950.
5. Von Bertalanffy, Ludwig. An Outline of General System Theory. The British Journal for the Philosophy of Science, Vol. 1, No. 2, pp. 134-165. 1950.

2. Today's Problems

1. Meadows, Donella. Thinking in Systems: A primer. Chelsea Green Publishing. 2008.

3. Quick Systems Overview

1. Lynn, Bryan. Many US States Struggle with Teacher Shortages. Learning English. 2018. https://learningenglish.voanews.com/a/many-us-states-struggle-with-teacher-shortages/4537983.html

2. Darling-Hammond, Linda. Inequality in Teaching and Schooling: How Opportunity Is Rationed to Students of Color in America NCBI. 2001. https://www.ncbi.nlm.nih.gov/books/NBK223640/

3. Stover, Del. Addressing teacher turnover in high-poverty, high-minority urban schools. NSBA. 2017. https://www.nsba.org/newsroom/addressing-teacher-turnover-high-poverty-high-minority-urban-schools

4. Volz, Matt. Fired pregnant teacher settles with Montana Catholic school. The Boston Globe. 2016. https://www.bostonglobe.com/news/nation/2016/03/15/fired-pregnant-teacher-settles-with-montana-catholic-school/ShlqaNHnaXXWO2HVUcDxiM/story.html

5. The Associated Press. Louisiana school has rescinded its hair extension ban after outcry, archdiocese says. CBC. 2018. https://www.cbc.ca/news/world/black-girl-hair-school-policy-extensions-1.4801371

6. Meadows, Donella. Thinking in Systems: A primer. Chelsea Green Publishing. 2008.

7. The second law of thermodynamics states that the total entropy of an isolated system can never decrease over time. The total entropy can remain constant in ideal cases where the system is in a steady state (equilibrium), or is undergoing a reversible process. From https://en.wikipedia.org/wiki/Second_law_of_thermodynamics

8. Von Bertalanffy, Ludwig. The Theory of Open Systems in Physics and Biology Science New Series, Vol. 111, No. 2872 (Jan. 13, 1950), pp. 23-29 Published by: American Association

for the Advancement of Science Stable URL: https://www.jstor.org/stable/1676073

4. Mental Models

1. Merritt, Jeremy. What Are Mental Models? The Systems Thinker. 2018. https://thesystemsthinker.com/what-are-mental-models/

2. Seonmin Kim, Victoria Jane Mabin, John Davies. The theory of constraints thinking processes: retrospect and prospect. International Journal of Operations & Production Management, Vol. 28 Issue: 2, pp.155-184. 2008. https://doi.org/10.1108/01443570810846883

3. Karash, Richard. Mental Models And Systems Thinking: Going Deeper Into Systemic Issues. The Systems Thinker. 2018. https://thesystemsthinker.com/mental-models-and-systems-thinking-going-deeper-into-systemic-issues/

4. Karash, Richard. Mental Models And Systems Thinking: Going Deeper Into Systemic Issues. The Systems Thinker. 2018. https://thesystemsthinker.com/mental-models-and-systems-thinking-going-deeper-into-systemic-issues/

5. *Diagram 7*. Original picture from Karash, Richard. Mental Models And Systems Thinking: Going Deeper Into Systemic Issues. The Systems Thinker. 2018. https://thesystemsthinker.com/mental-models-and-systems-thinking-going-deeper-into-systemic-issues/

6. Karash, Richard. Mental Models And Systems Thinking: Going Deeper Into Systemic Issues. The Systems Thinker. 2018. https://thesystemsthinker.com/mental-models-and-systems-thinking-going-deeper-into-systemic-issues/

7. Karash, Richard. Goodman, Michael R. Going Deeper: Moving from Understanding to Action. Applied Systems Thinking. 1995.

http://www.appliedsystemsthinking.com/supporting_docu
ments/PracticeGoingDeeper.pdf

5. Systems Essentials

1. Newswire. Ramapough Mountain Indians Sue Ford Over Toxic Contamination. Newswire. 2006. http://www.ens-newswire.com/ens/jan2006/2006-01-21-01.html

2. Bregel, Emily. Fog-induced wreck prompted lawsuits. Times Free Press. 2010. https://www.timesfreepress.com/news/news/story/2010/dec/05/fog-induced-wreck-prompted-lawsuits/36307/

3. Strachan, Glenn. Systems Thinking. International Research Institute in Sustainability, University of Gloucestershire. 2018. http://arts.brighton.ac.uk/__data/assets/pdf_file/0004/5926/Systems-Thinking.pdf

4. Invasive Animals CRC. Introduction of the cane toad to Australia. Pest Smart. 2012. https://www.pestsmart.org.au/pestsmart-case-study-introduction-of-the-cane-toad-to-australia/

5. Sherwell, Philip. A plague of Burmese pythons in the Everglades. The Telegraph. 2009. https://www.telegraph.co.uk/news/worldnews/northamerica/usa/5956739/A-plague-of-Burmese-pythons-in-the-Everglades.html

6. Meadows, Donella. Thinking in Systems: A primer. Chelsea Green Publishing. 2008.

7. Frey, Rebecca Joyce. Genocide and International Justice. Facts On File. ISBN 978-0816073108. 2009.

8. Pilkington, Ed. Robin Wright targets Congo's 'conflict minerals' violence with new campaign. The Guardian. 2016. https://www.theguardian.com/world/2016/may/17/robin-wright-stand-with-congo-campaign-mining-house-of-cards

9. Integrated Taxonomy Information System. https://www.itis.gov

10. Geoff W Adams, The Emperor Commodus : gladiator, Hercules or a tyrant?. Boca Raton: BrownWalker Press. ISBN 1612337228. 2013.

11. Aronson, Daniel. Overview of Systems Thinking. Daniel Aronson. 1996. http://www.thinking.net/Systems_Thinking/OverviewSTarticle.pdf

12. *Diagram 8*. Original picture from Aronson, Daniel. Overview of Systems Thinking. Daniel Aronson. 1996. Retrieved in 2018. http://www.thinking.net/Systems_Thinking/OverviewSTarticle.pdf

13. Aronson, Daniel. Overview of Systems Thinking. Daniel Aronson. 1996. http://www.thinking.net/Systems_Thinking/OverviewSTarticle.pdf

14. *Diagram 9*. Original picture from Aronson, Daniel. Overview of Systems Thinking. Daniel Aronson. 1996. http://www.thinking.net/Systems_Thinking/OverviewSTarticle.pdf

15. Aronson, Daniel. Overview of Systems Thinking. Daniel Aronson. 1996. http://www.thinking.net/Systems_Thinking/OverviewSTarticle.pdf

16. Meadows, Donella. Thinking in Systems: A primer. Chelsea Green Publishing. 2008.

17. Forrester, Jay. Collected Papers of Jay Forrester. Jay Forrester. Pegasus Communications. 1975.

18. Meadows, Donella. Thinking in Systems: A primer. Chelsea Green Publishing. 2008.

6. Examples Of One And Two-Stock Systems

1. *Diagram 10*. Original picture from Thinking in Systems: A primer. Chelsea Green Publishing. 2008.

2. Meadows, Donella. Thinking in Systems: A primer. Chelsea Green Publishing. 2008.

3. *Diagram 11*. Original picture from Thinking in Systems: A primer. Chelsea Green Publishing. 2008.

4. Meadows, Donella. Thinking in Systems: A primer. Chelsea Green Publishing. 2008.

5. Meadows, Donella. Thinking in Systems: A primer. Chelsea Green Publishing. 2008.

6. *Diagram 12*. Original picture from Thinking in Systems: A primer. Chelsea Green Publishing. 2008.

7. Chatteerjee, Pratap. Dick Cheney's Halliburton: a corporate case study. The Guardian. 2011. https://www.theguardian.com/commentisfree/cifamerica/2011/jun/08/dick-cheney-halliburton-supreme-court

7. Systems Archetypes

1. I See Systems. Applying Systems Thinking and Common Archetypes to Organizational Issues. Module 6: Systems Archetypes. 2018. https://www.iseesystems.com/Online_training/course/module6/6-02-0-0-what.htm

2. Meadows, Donella. Thinking in Systems: A primer. Chelsea Green Publishing. 2008.

3. Hale, David M. Behind the bling: The story of Clemson's epic championship rings. ESPN. 2017. http://www.espn.com/college-football/story/_/id/20466841/clemson-tigers-dabo-swinney-big-business-college-football-championship-rings

4. *Diagram 13*. Original Picture from I See Systems. Applying Systems Thinking and Common Archetypes to Organizational Issues. Module 6: Systems Archetypes. Implications & Leverage Points. Success to the Successful. I See Systems. 2018. https://www.iseesystems.com/Online_training/course/module6/6-13-3-0-successimp.htm

5. Herbert, Christopher E. Haurin , Donald R. Rosenthal, Stuart S. Duda, Mark. Homeownership Gaps Among Low-Income and Minority Borrowers and Neighborhoods. U.S. Department

of Housing and Urban Development. 2005. https://www.huduser.gov/Publications/pdf/HomeownershipGapsAmong Low-IncomeAndMinority.pdf

6. Beattie, Andrwe. Why Buying in Bulk Doesn't Always Save You Money. Investopedia. 2018. https://www.investopedia.com/articles/pf/07/bulk_buying.asp

7. *Diagram 14*. Original picture from I See Systems. Applying Systems Thinking and Common Archetypes to Organizational Issues. Module 6: Systems Archetypes. Implications & Leverage Points. Success to the Successful. I See Systems. 2018. https://www.iseesystems.com/Online_training/course/module6/6-13-3-0-successimp.htm

8. I See Systems. Applying Systems Thinking and Common Archetypes to Organizational Issues. Module 6: Systems Archetypes. Implications & Leverage Points. Success to the Successful. I See Systems. 2018. https://www.iseesystems.com/Online_training/course/module6/6-13-3-0-successimp.htm

9. *Diagram 15*. I See Systems. Original picture from Applying Systems Thinking and Common Archetypes to Organizational Issues. Module 6: Systems Archetypes. Implications & Leverage Points. Escalation. I See Systems. 2018. https://www.iseesystems.com/Online_training/course/module6/6-11-3-0-escalimp.htm

10. Meadows, Donella. Thinking in Systems: A primer. Chelsea Green Publishing. 2008.

11. *Diagram 16*. Original picture from I See Systems. Applying Systems Thinking and Common Archetypes to Organizational Issues. Module 6: Systems Archetypes. Implications & Leverage Points. Shifting the Burden. I See Systems. 2018. https://www.iseesystems.com/Online_training/course/module6/6-06-3-0-shiftimp.htm

12. I See Systems. Applying Systems Thinking and Common Archetypes to Organizational Issues. Module 6: Systems Archetypes. Implications & Leverage Points. Shifting the

Burden. I See Systems. 2018. https://www.iseesystems.com/Online_training/course/module6/6-06-3-0-shiftimp.htm

8. Systems Thinking in Social Matters

1. Stroh, Peter David. Systems Thinking For Social Change. Chelsea Green Publishing. 2015.

2. Onda, Tsuyoshi. Abortion Worldwide 2017: Uneven Progress and Unequal Access. Guttmacher. 2018. https://www.guttmacher.org/report/abortion-worldwide-2017

3. Death Penalty Information Center. Deterrence: States Without the Death Penalty Have Had Consistently Lower Murder Rates. Death Penalty Information Center. 2017. https://deathpenaltyinfo.org/deterrence-states-without-death-penalty-have-had-consistently-lower-murder-rates

4. Stroh, Peter David. Systems Thinking For Social Change. Chelsea Green Publishing. 2015.

5. Collaboration for Impact. The Collective Impact Framework. Collaboration for Impact. 2018.

6. Stroh, Peter David. Systems Thinking For Social Change. Chelsea Green Publishing. 2015.

7. *Diagram 17*. Original picture from Northwest Earth Institute. A Systems Thinking Model: The Iceberg. Northwest Earth Institute. 2018. https://www.nwei.org/iceberg/

8. Gerber, John. Systems Thinking Tools: Finding The Root Cause(S) Of Big Problems. Changing The Story. 2012. https://changingthestory.net/2012/07/18/rootcaus/

9. Northwest Earth Institute. A Systems Thinking Model: The Iceberg. Northwest Earth Institute. 2018. https://www.nwei.org/iceberg/

10. Durose, Matthew. Cooper, Alexia D. Ph.D., Snyder, Howard N. Ph.D. Recidivism of Prisoners Released in 30 States in 2005: Patterns from 2005 to 2010. U.S. Department of Justice. 2014. https://www.bjs.gov/content/pub/pdf/rprts05p0510.pdf

11. Pryser Libell, Henrik. Anders Behring Breivik, Killer in 2011 Norway Massacre, Says Prison Conditions Violate His Rights. The New York Times. 2016. https://www.nytimes.com/2016/03/16/world/europe/anders-breivik-nazi-prison-lawsuit.html

12. Sterbenz, Christina. Why Norway's prison system is so successful. Business Insider. 2014. https://www.businessinsider.com/why-norways-prison-system-is-so-successful-2014-12/?IR=T

13. World Prison Brief. Highest to Lowest. Prison Population Total. World Prison Brief. 2018. http://www.prisonstudies.org/highest-to-lowest/prison-population-total?field_region_taxonomy_tid=All

14. Martin, Will. The 31 safest countries in the world. Business Insider. 2018. https://www.businessinsider.my/safest-countries-in-the-world-2018-6/?r=US&IR=T

15. Stroh, Peter David. Systems Thinking For Social Change. Chelsea Green Publishing. 2015.

16. Kubish C, Anne. Structural Racism. Racial Equity Tools. 2006. www.racialequitytools.org/resourcefiles/kubisch.pdf   [URL inactive]

9. A Comprehensive Study on Systems Thinking and a Social Issue

1. Stroh, Peter David. Goodman, Michael. A Systemic Approach to Ending Homelessness. Applied Systems Thinking. 2007. http://www.appliedsystemsthinking.com/supporting_documents/TopicalHomelessness.pdf

2. Stroh, Peter David. Goodman, Michael. A Systemic Approach to Ending Homelessness. Applied Systems Thinking. 2007. http://www.appliedsystemsthinking.com/supporting_documents/TopicalHomelessness.pdf

3. *Diagram 19*. Original picture from Stroh, Peter David. Goodman, Michael. A Systemic Approach to Ending Homelessness.

Applied Systems Thinking. 2007. http://www.appliedsystems-thinking.com/supporting_documents/TopicalHomelessness.pdf

4. Stroh, Peter David. Goodman, Michael. A Systemic Approach to Ending Homelessness. Applied Systems Thinking. 2007. http://www.appliedsystemsthinking.com/supporting_docu-ments/TopicalHomelessness.pdf

5. Zurcher, Kathleen. Stroh, Peter David. Acting and Thinking Systemically. The Systems Thinker. 2018. https://thesystems-thinker.com/acting-and-thinking-systemically/

6. Battle Creek Michigan. Homeless Coalition discusses local facts on health fair day. Battle Creek Michigan. 2017. https://www.battlecreekmi.gov/CivicAlerts.aspx?AID=505&ARC=624

7. Stroh, Peter David. Systems Thinking For Social Change. Chelsea Green Publishing. 2015.

10. Exercises

1. Collen, Arne. Minati, Gianfranco. Seven Activities To Engage Systems Thinking. Semantic Scholar. 1997. https://pdfs.seman ticscholar.org/3436/c52688ab6dae545fdb783bb0b88b8b052c16.pdf

2. Collen, Arne. Minati, Gianfranco. Seven Activities To Engage Systems Thinking. Semantic Scholar. 1997. https://pdfs.seman ticscholar.org/3436/c52688ab6dae545fdb783bb0b88b8b052c16.pdf

3. Booth Sweeney, Linda. Meadows, Dennis. The Systems Thinking Playbook. Chelsea Green Publishing. 2010.

4. Booth Sweeney, Linda. Meadows, Dennis. The Systems Thinking Playbook. Chelsea Green Publishing. 2010.

Afterword

1. Meadows, Donella. Thinking in Systems: A primer. Chelsea Green Publishing. 2008.
2. Stroh, Peter David. Systems Thinking For Social Change. Chelsea Green Publishing. 2015.

Made in the USA
Monee, IL
10 December 2024

73110872R00144